PRAISE FOR EXPLORING CAMPUS DIVERSITY: CASE STUDIES AND EXERCISES

"*Exploring Campus Diversity: Case Studies and Exercises* is an important, timely book that all academics should read. It provides keen insight into the many complex issues related to cultural diversity on American college campuses, and it offers readers the opportunity to think through that complexity by considering real-world cases."
—**Dr. Christopher P. Campbell**, editor of *The Routledge Companion to Media and Race*; coauthor of *Race and News: Critical Perspectives*; and author of *Race, Myth and the News*

"*Exploring Campus Diversity* engages the issues of diversity, equity, and inclusive excellence in creative and engaging ways that position both faculty and college students to critically undertake difficult conversations around equity, diversity, and inclusivity. It is a promising tool for academic discourse that informs, educates, and shapes perspectives and worldviews for life in the twenty-first-century global society. Strongly recommended for schools and colleges!"
—**Dr. Chinaka S. DomNwachukwu**, professor of multicultural education and associate dean for Accreditation, School of Education, Azusa Pacific University; author of *The Theory and Practice of Multicultural Education* and *An Introduction to Multicultural Education: From Theory to Practice*

"As many universities work toward inclusive excellence on their campuses, it is important that they establish a culture that is safe, open to productive dialogue, and welcoming to those from all backgrounds. This book is a useful tool in establishing that culture. Through the use of case studies, incoming students will really think about what it means for people from all walks of life and with various perspectives to share a campus community. They will get useful tips and tools to help them navigate conversations and interactions across difference."
—**Dr. Kim M. LeDuff**, vice president of academic engagement and chief diversity officer, University of West Florida

Exploring Campus Diversity

OTHER BOOKS BY THE EDITORS

Coping with Gender Inequities: Critical Conversations of Women Faculty (Thompson and Parry)
Encyclopedia of Diversity and Social Justice (Thompson)
Encyclopedia of Diversity and Social Justice, Two Volumes (Thompson)

Exploring Campus Diversity

Case Studies and Exercises

Edited by Sherwood Thompson and Pam Parry

ROWMAN & LITTLEFIELD
Lanham • Boulder • New York • London

Published by Rowman & Littlefield
An imprint of The Rowman & Littlefield Publishing Group, Inc.
4501 Forbes Boulevard, Suite 200, Lanham, Maryland 20706
www.rowman.com

6 Tinworth Street, London SE11 5AL, United Kingdom

British Library Cataloguing in Publication Information Available

Library of Congress Cataloging-in-Publication Data Is Available

978-1-4758-3502-1 (cloth: alk. paper)
978-1-4758-3503-8 (pbk: alk. paper
978-1-4758-3504-5 (electronic)

∞™ The paper used in this publication meets the minimum requirements of American National Standard for Information Sciences—Permanence of Paper for Printed Library Materials, ANSI/NISO Z39.48-1992.

Printed in the United States of America

We dedicate this book to our past, present, and future students in the hope that they will choose to be change agents and forge a path to greater human relations, accepting the presence of diverse racial, cultural, economic, and social groups. We dedicate this book to those who are standing on the shoulders of giants and lifting the torch of enlightenment for generations to come.

Contents

Foreword

Sara Zeigler

When I learned that Sherwood Thompson and Pam Parry planned to co-edit *Exploring Campus Diversity*, a series of case studies about some of the most challenging issues confronting thoughtful academics, I was eager to see the manuscript. Drs. Thompson and Parry are longtime colleagues of mine, both of whom have taught at Eastern Kentucky University and navigated intersectionality and marginalization as teachers, administrators, colleagues, and friends.

Both share a profound commitment to creating an inclusive and respectful environment that recognizes the dignity of every individual in the campus community, but also to confronting bias, to intellectual inquiry, to courageous and academically rigorous classroom discussions, and to bringing emotionally sensitive issues into the open. Dr. Thompson has worked as a chief diversity officer and assistant dean and has played a prominent role in critical discussions about diversity. Dr. Parry illustrated these principles as a department chair and teacher, guiding colleagues and students through challenging discussions with compassion.

The values that Drs. Thompson and Parry brought to their own work are reflected in the work you are about to read. As a dean, a professor of political science, a former department chair, and a former Title IX coordinator, I've seen students struggle with all elements of identity. I've heard stories of discrimination based on the elements raised in this text, and I've faced my own biases, many of which were so deeply buried that I was unaware of them until they surfaced upon conducting an interview or facing a student who felt hurt by a comment that was unexpected and unintentionally offensive.

As you consider the multiple elements of diversity that we encounter, respect, and welcome on the 21st-century campus, also consider what you hope to inculcate in the students who graduate from institutions of higher learning and in the citizens who will emerge and become leaders. We cannot expect a world without bias, without stereotyping, or without misunderstanding. If we, as educators, do our work well, we will graduate students who constantly challenge their own opinions, who interact with others fearlessly and effectively, and who recognize and correct for their own biases.

Exploring Campus Diversity provides educators with tools for initiating thought-provoking conversations in multiple contexts. It offers a rich array of topical scenarios, with subject matter ranging from classroom management to the feminization/masculinization of professions, to First Amendment concerns, to disability accommodation, to language acquisition, and to effective allyship. Each scenario is brief enough to be read and understood in a normal class session and is accompanied by discussion questions appropriate for either an in-class discussion or a more in-depth discussion board or essay assignment. The level is appropriate for the beginning college student and provides the opportunity for the instructor to introduce concepts of identity to the class or to delve into more advanced work in intersectionality, implicit bias, and privilege as the skills and maturity of the students permit.

A particularly nice feature of the book is its willingness to present faculty members and administrators as flawed and complex beings who also struggle to manage diversity, even when well intentioned. For example, Doris W. Carroll's piece, "Can Online Teaching Be Inclusive?," presents a faculty member who both marginalizes by showing impatience with the student's need for accommodations, but who also shows great deftness in managing a discussion board that turns hostile. This nuanced portrayal of a professor is both realistic and reassuring—most faculty members make mistakes in managing the classroom climate, and most of us also do well. It is a refreshing departure from the usual practice to see a single character engage in discriminatory behavior and in allyship in the same scenario and a recognition of the reality of the human experience.

Some scenarios move beyond the campus to confront some highly intractable problems of our day. Willie R. Tubbs provides a case study about flags that incorporate Confederate symbolism, allowing a starting point for conversations about how to manage aspects of history that have been popularized and adopted as symbols or mascots and integrated into traditions. The case focuses on the campus context but can lead to much larger conversations about monuments, statutes, and even the very names of buildings and institutions. Tubbs also grapples with the challenge of diversity at Christian campuses (principles that can be extrapolated to other contexts) and how one reconciles the right of private colleges to the free exercise of religion to the values of respect and tolerance for all.

Exploring Campus Diversity is an outstanding resource for the educator who seeks to initiate thought-provoking and nuanced discussions of diversity in classrooms on her or his campus—or who simply wants to think more deeply about diversity in all of its incarnations.

Sara Zeigler, Ph.D.
Dean, College of Letters, Arts, and Social Sciences
Eastern Kentucky University

Acknowledgments

There are always dedicated and passionate individuals behind every endeavor that reaches out to help students acquire skills to live in a diverse society, composed of individuals from many different ethnicities, religions, ages, sexualities, and physical abilities. Many of those individuals assisted us in the composition of this book.

This book would not have been possible without the cooperation, assistance, and support of the authors who contributed to this book project. We are indebted to our professional colleagues who reviewed and shared their comments about the content of the book. Special thanks go to Southeast Missouri State University student Alex Bargen for proofreading the manuscript—an extra set of eyes is always welcome.

Appreciation is expressed to the members of the editorial staff of Rowman & Littlefield for their guidance during this process. We are particularly grateful to our families for their patience and support.

Introduction

Sherwood Thompson

There was a great outcry among some social scientists after the election in 2008 of President Barack H. Obama, declaring that the United States has finally reached a postracial society status after more than 200 years of history. Television appearances of social critics, newly published books, and radio talk show hosts claimed that the United States was headed on track toward a new society where race is no longer significant.

This new reality was short-lived, and of course, it became apparent to many that instead of a postracial society, in fact, after President Obama's presidency, there was a lingering culture of resentment among White nationalists, Alt-right groups, and far-right ideologues, who declare White identity as a superior culture and multiculturalism as a political-correctness plot.

College and university students are bombarded with these terms and are confronted with organizers who try to recruit them as members of these groups. There is an increasing number of student-recognized student organizations on college and university campuses. Each student group has its mission and philosophy. These organizations offer students an opportunity to become engaged in campus life while helping them to meet and make friends with individuals from different cultures and backgrounds.

There has been, however, an increasing number of White Student Union clubs established on college and university campuses with the expressed mission to practice separation and division. Students should be free to choose what type of organizational affiliation they want to associate with and be a member of. Nevertheless, they should have an awareness of which organization will give them the best experiences that will augment their overall college or university training. Students should be able to select friends who will also complement their academic goals in life and not weigh them down with mixed messages that are unpopular and contradictory.

As more diverse populations arrive on college and university campuses, administrators and faculty have begun to pay increasing attention to the need to offer diversity orientation and training courses to new students. Diversity orientation classes that explore diversity themes, global awareness, service learning, and social justice have become commonplace on most public university and college campuses. The goal of understanding the campus climate is the first step in these classes for new students.

Exploring Campus Diversity: Case Studies and Exercises provides a resource for diversity-themed classes. It offers a rich prospective for the reader to become engaged in discussions with diverse peers positively in a formal classroom setting or online. Although social class interaction might skew how different students' worldview of society is, the case studies in this book are crafted to engage all students across social classes to interact and share their opinion and personal experiences regarding the impact diversity has had on their lives regardless of their place in society.

This book will generate new ways of thinking and new viewpoints on the values and cultural capital that individuals bring to a campus environment—their attitudes, personal experiences, language, traditions, insights, and how they interact among and between different cultural groups.

Exploring Campus Diversity: Case Studies and Exercises examines the realistic chain of events that occur on college and university campuses across the United States, involving issues of diversity and campus climate. To that end, this book offers case studies alongside probing questions designed to provoke discussions on issues of diversity and campus climate. The scenarios presented in this book strive to deeply investigate the standard base of knowledge surrounding diversity in higher education through their personal experience and their studies of cultural differences.

Specifically, *Exploring Campus Diversity: Case Studies and Exercises* investigates situations that reflect the challenges of expanding diversity and equity on college and university campuses. Each case study offers an everyday example of a potential problem that a college or university might encounter when grappling with diversity and campus climate issues. Each narrative is followed by problem-solving questions that aim to guide readers into new ways of thinking about diversity scenarios and addressing the diversity dilemma.

This book features contributions from practicing diversity experts and educators who will serve as content authors offering examples of case studies to help illuminate the issues that must be confronted by institutions' leaders and policy makers. These experts are from throughout the United States, and they have had years of experience working with diverse student groups trying to promote cultural competence and diversity and inclusion awareness.

This book's ultimate goal is to provoke wide-ranging, yet focused discussions that resist oversimplifying the diversity conversation. It is not the intention of this book to tell the reader what to think but to engage the reader in deep and critical thinking about diversity issues. Together, the contributions underscore that higher education cannot just ignore the challenges of diversity and campus complacency, nor can it be content to lay blame on the broader society.

Diversity, especially at the postsecondary level, is a topic that needs multifaceted perspectives and viewpoints from different cultural backgrounds and a commitment from all members of the academic community to come to a consensus on the appreciation and understanding of diversity and civility. To this end, this book presents provocative and thoughtful perspectives that demonstrate how inclusive learning environments deal with the acceptance, affirmation, contribution, inclusion, interaction, and participation of diverse populations.

These case studies are real-life situations and they apply to a broad range of social-learning approaches offering the reader in-depth analyses of particular scenarios where an individual can take the opportunity to contextualize and reflect on the diversity and campus climate issues presented. With its array of learning activities, the book serves as an intersection of critiques, reflections, and personal experiences involving relevant real-world scenarios.

Exploring Campus Diversity: Case Studies and Exercises will specifically examine diversity challenges on college and university campuses and provide students with the opportunity to learn how diversity issues are being addressed by institutional administrators, faculty, and students. As the United States undergoes increasing demographic shifts, all members of the campus community must contend with issues of access, affordability, gender equality, race-conscious admission policies, and global interaction among international student communities. This reality is noted by researchers, including the Pew Research Center, which shows that by the year 2055, the United States will not have a single racial or ethnic majority (Cohn & Caumant, 2016).

The book openly discusses the different challenges that students will face and the ones that campus leaders will have to confront that drive institutional responses to diversity on both public and private campuses, showcasing how institutes of higher education waver between good-faith efforts at building diverse learning communities and rigidly maintaining the status quo.

One excellent feature of this book is the collection of content authors from across the United States who have worked to advance diversity on college and university campuses. These contributing authors provide compelling accounts of campus diversity case studies based on their own experiences and observations that allow readers to explore real-life situations and discover new ways of understanding the variable dimensions of diversity on college and university campuses. This book further advances the conversation of diversity on campuses, eliminating the tendency to provide lip service to the issue. It gives readers an appropriate forum to discuss heated diversity issues in an environment that is free from criticism.

Exploring Campus Diversity: Case Studies and Exercises is a book that contains 38 case studies carefully selected to reflect topics that are commonplace on college and university campuses. This book presents a fresh and timely perspective on an array of diversity and campus climate topics and covers ethical issues from a practical perspective.

A few books on the market presently address the experiences and relationships of students dealing with diversity issues on campuses in a case study format. This book will allow readers to probe specific matters about diversity, reflect on discussion questions, analyze each case by the authors, and draw conclusions from information and assertions made about case study theme. *Exploring Campus Diversity: Case Studies and Exercises* will generate and allow for lively discussions that will promote an exchange of views by the reader on diversity issues that challenge higher education.

REFERENCE

Cohn, D., & Caumant, A. (2106). *10 demographic trends that are shaping the U.S. and the world*. Retrieved from http://www.pewresearch.org/fact-tank/2016/03/31/10-demographic-trends-that-are-shaping-the-u-s-and-the-world/

UNIT 1
CAMPUS CLIMATE

ONE

Questioning the Right to Protest

Taking a Knee at the
Homecoming Football Game

Sherwood Thompson

It was a mild and sunny fall Saturday afternoon. Fans of the hometown and opposing teams packed the stadium. The home team was getting ready to play its homecoming game with a very impressive record of division wins. A homecoming victory would undoubtedly guarantee a trip to a bowl game.

Robert, the star quarterback, an African-American athlete recruited from Mississippi, was expected by all accounts to break the school record for rushing and passing. He had been the hero in previous games, and because of his successful record, the local fans celebrated him as their hope for taking the team to new heights. The crowd was electric and was anticipating a "good game."

When the announcer asked the crowd to stand for the playing of the national anthem, the fans were aghast to witness that over half of the football players, including the star quarterback, were kneeling on the sideline. The fans couldn't understand why this was happening, especially on such an important homecoming game day. Before the game, the players made up their minds that they would express their support for the ongoing national protest movement bringing attention to the senseless killing and violence that African Americans were experiencing at the hands of White police officers.

"Taking a knee" is a football strategy used by teams when a quarterback kneels to the ground, ending the play on contact, after receiving the snap (Marlin, 2006). Taking a knee is tantamount to saying that the game is over. In the context of a protest, former San Francisco 49ers quarterback Colin Kaepernick popularized the use of this symbol. His kneeling on the sideline was originally intended to express solidarity with Black Lives Matter, a movement to bring attention to the injustices of urban Black youth and all people of color (Branigin, 2017).

Kaepernick's action prompted many other NFL players to take a knee on the sidelines during the national anthem to protest police brutality and hostility experienced mainly by African-American males. Their action sends the message similar to the quarterback kneeling on the field when a ball is grounded, that it's time to end the violence.

Many African-American male victims have suffered bloodshed or death at the hands of the police, and the majority of the police officers who perpetrated the violence up to this writing have been acquitted of their wrongdoing (Associated Press, 2009; Lee, 2017; Politi, 2015; Smith, 2016). In 2015, the most alarming year of data collection on African-American killings by police officers, the number of African-American deaths were 1,134 (Swaine, Laughland, Larley, & McCarthy, 2015).

When Robert participated in taking a knee with his teammates on the sideline, many in the stadium booed, jeered, and shouted insults to the players and particularly singled out Robert by name. These emotional reactions were so disturbing to Robert that he later told a friend that he just wanted to quit and go home.

But, as expected, Robert broke two school records for passing and rushing, and his teammates advanced to win the homecoming game, which assured them a spot in the upcoming bowl game in their division.

After the game, the athletic director summoned Robert to his office. Robert had never been asked before to join in a meeting after a game. After most games, win or lose, Robert and his teammates would share a hearty meal and then just hang out; but this time something was different. Robert brushed his negative feeling aside and thought maybe the athletic director just wanted to congratulate him for a game well played.

Upon reaching the office he saw reporters in the hallway, and upon entering the room, he was surprised to see the president of the university, the head football coach, the athletic director, someone from the legal council's office, and the campus chief of police. They were not in a celebratory mood—no smiles. Robert thought to himself: I wonder what this is all about.

Robert took a seat, and before he could ask what the nature of the meeting was, the athletic director quickly informed him that he would be suspended from the team immediately and not allowed to play in the upcoming bowl game. The coach reluctantly spoke up and told Robert that his athletic scholarship would be revoked and he would no longer be welcomed as a member of the team. The president just looked away and said nothing.

Robert was speechless. He got up and headed for the door and ran down the hallway in anger, speaking to no one as he exited the building. His teammates were waiting for him in the lobby of his residence hall. They realized that something was wrong with Robert. They tried to hug him and give him high fives, but Robert shoved them off. In a soft tone, Robert told his friends about his fate. Everyone was somber. Robert spoke up again and said, "Even at my university with all that I have contributed, my career has been murdered."

FRAMING THE PROBLEM

Coming from Mississippi, Robert was well aware of the harmful impact racism has on African-American people. He had relatives who told him about the night riders, hangings, and the repeated discrimination directed toward African Americans in Mississippi. While many of these incidents happened long before Robert was born, he recalled the cruel stories and pledged, at a young age, not to become a victim of such ruthlessness. He decided to make his mark in football and to be a high-achieving athlete.

Living in a small, rural university town, Robert encountered many incidents in the local White community; however, when individuals noticed that he was the university's star quarterback, they softened their tone and their insults. His African-American friends were not as lucky when being confronted by racial hostility. They would always decry how difficult it was to get a job in the local businesses or how at night they were often followed by the city police for no apparent reason.

Robert and his African-American friends always questioned why their White counterparts who were seemingly sensitive to issues of intolerance never said or did anything about it. Robert pondered his situation and wanted to know why if nearly half of the football team, African Americans, Latinos, and Whites alike, took a knee, then why was he the only one to be dismissed from the team?

Stemming from Kaepernick's protest, NFL fans' behavior varied from burning sports gear to police officers refusing to work security at games (CNN Wire, 2017). Robert thought that maybe the local fans would be more open-minded about this symbolic gesture of taking a knee. He never imagined that they would react like those fans of the NFL. Robert evidently thought that his fans and the university administrators were empathic to the purpose of the protest. Why shouldn't they support the elimination of racial inequality and bigotry? Robert had no idea that people in this university town, despite some discriminatory practices, would react the way they did.

Robert was treated in a very demeaning manner—disrespected and misunderstood. He was humiliated in front of the same individuals who often congratulated him for his performance on the field. He felt as if he was being used by the university to bring notoriety but not being appreciated by university officials for his beliefs. Robert surmised that the university environment did not live up to its mission of diversity and social justice. Like the police officers that he protested against for killing African Americans, the university officials were guilty of murdering his dreams.

DISCUSSION QUESTIONS

1. Do you think that the First Amendment to the United States Constitution protects individuals who want to take a knee in protest?
2. Was it proper for the university administrators to hold a meeting about Robert's decision to take a knee immediately after the winning football game? Why or why not?
3. If you were the football coach, and your star player had just clinched a spot in an upcoming bowl game for the university, would you make an effort to negotiate with the university administration to be lenient with Robert?
4. As a player on the same team as Robert, do you believe you have a responsibility to support Robert? And if so, in what ways could you and your teammates help him?
5. What role should the faculty play, if any, in supporting Robert's right to protest?
6. Does the university have a responsibility to teach and expose students to issues of diversity and social justice? Why or why not?

Editors' Note: *This hypothetical scenario does not reflect an actual student athlete or university officials, but rather this story represents the type of conflict that can occur when students engage in protest.*

REFERENCES

Associated Press. (2009). Retired Connecticut police officer Robert Lawlor acquitted of killing 2 unarmed black men. Retrieved from http://www.masslive.com/news/index.ssf/2009/12/retired_white_conn_police_offi.html

Branigin, A. (2017). Georgetown law professors will take a knee to protest Jeff Session's free speech visit. *The Root*. Retrieved from https://www.theroot.com/georgetown-law-professors-will-take-a-knee-to-protest-j-1818804065

CNN Wire. (2017). Backlash grows against players who take a knee during anthem. Retrieved from http://ktla.com/2017/09/27/backlash-grows-against-nfl-players-who-take-a-knee-during-anthem/

Lee, K. (2017). Former Arizona police officer acquitted in killing in fatal shooting captured on body camera. *Los Angeles Times.* Retrieved from http://www.latimes.com/nation/la-na-mesa-arizona-police-shooting-20171208-story.html.

Marlin, B. (2006). Taking a knee. *Urban Dictionary.* Retrieved from https://www.urbandictionary.com/define.php?term=take%20a%20knee.

Politi, D. (2015). Cleveland police officer acquitted for firing 15 shots that killed unarmed black couple. Retrieved from http://www.slate.com/blogs/the_slatest/2015/05/23/michael_brelo_cleveland_police_officer_acquitted_for_killing_unarmed_black.html

Smith, M. (2016). Minnesota officer acquitted in killing of Philando Castile. Retrieved from https://www.nytimes.com/2017/06/16/us/police-shooting-trial-philando-castile.html

Swaine, J., Laughland, O., Larley, J., & McCarthy, C. (2015). Young black men killed by U.S. police at highest rate in year of 1,134 deaths. *The Guardian.* Retrieved from https://www.theguardian.com/us-news/2015/dec/31/the-counted-police-killings-2015-young-black-men

TWO

Did Stereotyping Cause a Terrible Case of Mistaken Identity?

Sherwood Thompson

At a midwestern liberal arts college, the campus police chief came to my residential hall and requested to see Alfred, an African-American male and senior at the school. When the residential director escorted Alfred to the front lobby, the police chief handed him an envelope. Alfred opened the envelope with the chief and director both standing there, and to his surprise, he read that he was to vacate the residential hall immediately.

Alfred was stunned by the news. He asked the chief what he had done to bring on the eviction. The residential director told Alfred to visit the dean of students the next day for an explanation. Alfred responded that he had nowhere to go, nowhere to store his things. The police chief told Alfred that he could collect his belongings the next day, under the supervision of a police escort. The residential director had made arrangements for Alfred for one night at a local motel.

The police chief escorted Alfred to his room to collect some clothing and toiletries before driving him to the motel. Once inside the motel room, Alfred telephoned his father to tell him what had happened. His father promised to drive to campus early the next afternoon to speak with college officials.

Anxiety and nerves haunted Alfred throughout the night as he tried to reflect on what he possibly could have done to warrant this drastic action. Nothing came to mind, so he eventually dozed off into a fitful sleep.

The next morning, Alfred received a call from his father. His father told him that he had already talked to the dean of students and the campus legal counsel. Alfred was to remain in the hotel, and upon his father's arrival, they would go together to visit the dean of students. His father assured him that everything would be OK.

The next day, Alfred and his father met with Dean Wilson. Dean Wilson apologized for the inconvenience and explained that there had been a case of mistaken identity that caused the police chief to identify Alfred as a person of interest in an on-campus crime. Dean Wilson expressed her regrets and reassured Alfred's father that Alfred was an excellent student, active in student organizations, and a regular volunteer in the local community mentoring high school students at risk.

Alfred's father was disappointed with how the college handled the situation. In an embittered tone, he told the dean that an apology was not enough to settle this matter. He told the dean that he was going to seek an appropriate remedy for the wrong treatment his son experienced. When Alfred asked the dean when he would be allowed to move back into his residential hall, the dean assured him that he could return freely at any time.

As Alfred and his father were walking out of the office, Dean Wilson offered, "If it makes any difference, I can refund Alfred's residential fees for this semester." In an estranged tone, she told them that the college administration was very saddened by the mistake.

FRAMING THE PROBLEM

Alfred is a socially involved African-American male student with a friendly personality, who garners respect from faculty and administration. He was a victim of mistaken identity. A White male custodian had called the campus police and reported that he saw Alfred stealing something from the campus bookstore.

Without questioning Alfred regarding the charge, the campus police chief arrived at Alfred's residential hall, demanded to see him, and ordered him to vacate. The residential hall director had been briefed in advance, but he found the situation confusing. He knew Alfred to be a model student and very polite; still, the hall director had to follow orders.

Was this a cause of mistaken identity, or was it a case of prejudice and stereotyping?

DISCUSSION QUESTIONS

1. Based on the limited facts in this case study scenario, do you think it was necessary for the campus chief of police to come to Alfred's residential hall to vacate him from the premises?

2. Was it proper to keep information regarding his eviction from Alfred? What rights do you think Alfred has in a situation like this one?
3. Do you believe that the dean of students conducted herself professionally in the meeting with Alfred and his father? What more might she have done in a situation like this?
4. African-American males are often victims of stereotyping and unfair mistaken identity. Research indicates that African-American males are most often the victims of mistaken identity and stereotyping cases, more so than their White counterparts (Bradshaw, 2010, p. 1). Do you believe that mistaken identity cases that affect African-American males are an accident or the result of intentional prejudices and stereotypes?
5. Is it the responsibility of a college to expose and teach about diversity, social prejudice, stereotypes, and social justice? Or is it the personal responsibility of each student to search for information about social inequity and stereotypes?

Editors' Note: *This hypothetical scenario does not depict actual students or university personnel but rather represents the type of interactions that may occur on campuses across the country.*

REFERENCE

Bradshaw, F. (2010). *Stereotyping the black male in the U.S.* Retrieved from https://hubpages.com/politics/Stereotyping-the-Black-Male-in-the-US

THREE

A Case Study in "Belonging"

How First-Generation College Students Contribute to Campus Diversity

Kathy Previs

When it comes to diversity, people usually think about race, gender, ethnic background, sexuality, and religion. Some even think about socio-economic status, which is probably the most closely related to students who are the first in their families to attend college. As this case study demonstrates, these students contribute as much to campus diversity as the aforementioned groups of people. It is important to note that a first-generation college student can also be diverse in traditional categories of diversity, such as those mentioned above.

To better understand how first-generation college students contribute to a diverse campus, let's first discuss traits and trends of this group of students. A first-generation college student is defined as a student who is the first in his or her family to complete a college education. First-generation college students can be from upper-, middle-, or lower-class families, economically speaking, but most are from more economically disadvantaged families. First-generation college students make up about half of the college population in the United States, according to a 2010 study by the U.S. Department of Education; 30% of all entering first-year students are first in their families to attend college (First-Generation Foundation, 2017).

In addition to being financially disadvantaged, being a first-generation college student is "one of the most often cited predictors of higher education failure"; and first-generation college students are less likely to finish college when compared to students whose parents have a bachelor's degree (First-Generation Foundation, 2017). Furthermore, research indicates that more than 25% of first-generation lower-income college students leave after their first year—four times the dropout rate of higher-income, second-generation college students (First-Generation Foundation, 2017). Yet another characteristic of first-generation college students is that they are more likely to be older when they enter college and are more likely to be employed. As we know, the more hours a student works, the less she or he is on campus, and therefore the less likely she or he is to be and to feel a part of the campus community.

Given these characteristics, how do you suppose first-generation college students contribute to campus diversity?

To examine all of the different ways, let's look at a real-life example of a first-generation college student, Sydney, who is a junior majoring in communication at a midsize university in the southeastern part of the United States. As you read her story, think about ways her background can uniquely contribute to a college campus in terms of diversity.

"There are a few things that make me diverse in being a college student, all of which I am very proud of. First, since before the start of my college career in high school, I have always been backed with utmost support from my family because I was eligible for opportunities that they were not and I always showed great interest in taking advantage of them," Sydney explained. "My family always makes sure to praise me simply for trying my best, and for that reason, among many others, I have always been on the Dean's or President's List."

Sydney added that another quality about her being a first in her family to attend college is that she comes from a lower-middle-class background and has to work to be able to attend college. "Supporting myself financially and balancing school has taught me quite a bit [about] time management. In addition, there was no one in my family to pave the way for me. We figured everything out together: what to get for my dorm room, how to register for classes, how to take out loans for school. I'm glad that one day I will be able to aid my children with these processes, but it feels good to have navigated my own path. I honestly don't think I would be nearly as headstrong if I wasn't a first-generation student, and for that, I am forever independent and forever thankful."

Like any student, first-generation students feel the need to belong and to be a part of the campus—perhaps even more so than those who are not first-generation students because of their drive to succeed. They want to make their families proud that they accomplished something nobody else in their family had yet achieved.

But it is not always easy fitting in.

In her experience, Sydney described a time when she felt out of place being a first-generation college student:

The only time I can think of is when I got the itinerary for Panhellenic recruitment. I was so excited to rush and I had paid the fee over the summer after I graduated high school. I've always been a super-involved student, honor roll, varsity track, honors choir, drum line in the marching band, you name it. I was friends with everyone and close with my teachers. When I read the recruitment schedule and all the dress guidelines that had subjective adjectives like "cocktail dress" "but not too sexy," I was just nervous, scared, and I had no situations to compare that to in my life and my parents knew nothing about Greek life. I just never showed up. I felt pretty defeated, but since then I've made a great place for myself here . . . and I'm happy with what I've created for myself.

Like any student who overcomes everyday problems on campus, first-generation students learn to be self-sufficient and can take pride in their ability to learn to navigate the waters for which they had no instruction. Compare this to students who come from other countries and must figure out the ways of life in a new environment. Both groups of students have this in common, and both sets of students contribute to diversity.

As we learned from Sydney, there are several ways that first-generation college students contribute to diversity:

1. Family support. Most families of first-generation college students are economically disadvantaged, so since they can't offer money, they can offer support. This support often makes the difference between a student staying in college or dropping out after only a short time. These students bring a can-do attitude into the classroom as well as a determination and skill set that enables them to solve problems in creative ways.
2. Family pride. Families are proud of students for trying their best, encouraging them to excel. When that happens, students are motivated to make the Dean's List.
3. Must work to support themselves. As a result, they have a skill of time management in balancing work and academic activities. These students also bring their real-world experiences of work to the classroom, thereby contributing to the body of knowledge.
4. Have to figure things out on their own. As a result, they learn to be resourceful and independent, two important qualities for which employers look when hiring job candidates.

FRAMING THE PROBLEM

When describing a population, whether it be a country or a college campus, diversity is not limited to race, gender, ethnic background, sexuality, religion, and socioeconomic status. First-generation college students also contribute to the diversity of a university student body. These students bring a variety of skills to campus that differ from traditional students, thereby enabling others to learn from their backgrounds and experiences.

DISCUSSION QUESTIONS

1. Besides the reasons listed above, in what ways do you think first-generation college students contribute to campus diversity?
2. Think about the first-generation college students you know. Would you be able to tell they were the first in their family to attend college had they not told you?
3. Do you think having a sense of not belonging is limited to diverse students such as first-generation students and others discussed in this book?
4. Think about Sydney's story of where she felt out of place going to a Greek event on campus because she didn't know what to wear. What would you have done?

Editors' Note: This case study is based on the real experiences of a college student, whom we have simply named Sydney with no last name in order to protect the student's identity. The case study is shared with her permission.

REFERENCES

First-Generation Foundation. (2017). Retrieved from http://www.firstgeneration foundation.org/

Hodges, J. L. (1999). *The effects of first-generation status upon the first-year college success patterns of students attending an urban multi-campus community college.* ERIC Digest, ED474344

Payne, K. (N.d.). First-generation college students: Their challenges and the advising strategies that can help. Retrieved from https://dus.psu.edu/mentor/old/articles/070131kp.htm

FOUR

Islam under the Microscope

A Story of an International Student

Mustapha Jourdini

In a richly diverse United States, bigotry and discrimination against minority groups have been shockingly explicit in recent years. The appalling events in Charlottesville, Virginia, serve as a stark reminder of the not-so-proud history of racism against minorities, particularly against the Black community.

Is the strong resurgence of White nationalists behind the Charlottesville events a natural result of the election of a president who uses national security as a ploy to bar citizens of six Muslim countries from entering the United States? Haven't the tragic terrorist attacks of September 11, 2001, taught us anything about Islam and Muslims? How come citizens of countries from whence come Muslim extremists who committed and continue to commit terrorist attacks on Americans and Muslims are not subject to President Donald Trump's executive order to bar Iranians, Syrians, Sudanese, Libyans, Somalians, and Yemenis from entering the United States? What do we tell millions of Muslims who love the American culture and wish to pursue their higher education in the United States?

These questions were raised by Omar, an international Muslim student from North Africa, in Professor Thompson's world history course taught at a regional southeastern public university. Being a member of a minority group himself, Dr. Thompson didn't say anything but listened with a sympathetic heart and a grimacing face. Instead, he asked his mostly Caucasian students what they knew about Islam and Muslims.

Jonathan, a church-going Christian, volunteered, "It's the devil's religion. These people are taught to hate Americans. Our preacher at church told us that Islam is the anti-Christ. They worship the moon god."

Albeit saddened by the comment, Dr. Thompson didn't seek to correct Jonathan; instead, he asked what the rest of the class thought. A flurry of mixed reactions proceeded.

Mary, also a practicing Christian, chipped in, "I don't think Muslims are bad people. They, too, believe in one God. I had a school trip to a mosque and they were very kind and hospitable with me and my school mates. I think there is so much confusion and the media is the main culprit."

Sarah couldn't wait to share her raw feelings: "You know, Omar; it hurts to say, but until you and all Muslim people accept Jesus as your sole savior, you're going to hell." At this point, Sarah expressed concern for what appears to her as "lost Muslim souls." Jonathan and many other students nodded in approval with Sarah.

Sitting back in the corner of the class, Chris, another White student, who was raising his hand, waiting patiently for his turn to participate, emphatically blurted out, "It's us Americans who are ignorant. The media and politicians duped us. We are bombarded daily with images of terrorist attacks committed by ignorant Muslims. Muslims are not all the same. People of other religions also have committed crimes against humanity. I took a world religions course from an unbiased Christian professor, and I came to appreciate what Islam has offered to the world. I do believe it's a peaceful religion. Of course, a minority of extremist Muslims use the Holy Quran to justify their heinous crimes in the same way extremist Christians, Jews, Hindus, Atheists, and Buddhists use their scripture to commit ungodly harmful acts."

Omar, the international student, quipped in a shivering soft voice, "No, no, no, we don't worship the moon. We worship Allah. God in English. The same God that created all prophets from Adam to Jesus and Muhammad, peace be upon all of them."

After making a wistful sigh, Omar continued, "I feel ashamed of these barbaric acts against civilians and innocent people committed in the name of Islam. That's not what Islam teaches us."

Dr. Thompson felt very proud of these exchanges among his mostly first-year college students. He wisely advised that it was important to always examine facts and that passing frivolous judgments is dangerous. He also asked students to think critically about their sources of information because, as learners, they can only improve and succeed when they are able to sift through the myriad of information that's available in print and online to arrive at well-informed decisions.

FRAMING THE PROBLEM

Omar is an international Muslim student pursuing a bachelor's degree in fire and safety engineering. He feels that his Muslim identity and his country of origin have caused him to be singled out not only at airports, where he goes through "random checks," but also in college. While Dr. Thompson remained curious and objective throughout the discussion about Islam, most student remarks were based on common stereotypes magnified by some churches, politicians, media outlets, and fearmongers.

Were students' reactions based on sheer ignorance of Islam and Muslims or stereotypes and bigotry fueled by special interest groups who feel threatened and can make good business by attacking the second-largest world religion?

DISCUSSION QUESTIONS

1. Based on the limited facts in this case study scenario, was it fair to claim that Muslims are taught to hate Americans?
2. How should we respond to Omar's question about what to tell millions of Muslim students who would love to come to the United States for higher education?
3. Is it constitutional to use religion as a basis to discriminate against adherents of any religion?
4. If true Christianity teaches that we do unto others what we want them to do unto us, how do you feel about a preacher telling his congregation that Muslims worship the moon god and Islam is the devil's religion?
5. In what ways can taking courses in comparative religion or culture help us become more culturally competent world citizens?
6. Is the U.S. government hypocritical to bar citizens from Muslim countries with little or no natural resources and allow citizens from Muslim countries that are rich with natural resources to enter its borders?
7. What can we learn from international Muslim students in American colleges and universities?

Editors' Note: *This hypothetical scenario is based on the author's own experiences both as a student and professional in higher education. This story represents the type of debate that can occur on college and university campuses.*

FIVE

Failure to Thrive

Can Multiple Identities Cause Conflict?

Leah Robinson and De'Andrea Matthews

Prior to the start of classes in an accelerated Allied Health program, students were required to work together and come up with a module to learn and teach medical terminology. This group assignment was meant to examine their group dynamics, creative problem solving, and tap into self-directed learning. It was important that the students developed an orientation and understanding of medical terms before class started.

Before the student presentations began, Cristina told the instructor that she was not feeling well and excused herself to go to the bathroom. The instructor later learned that she had not gone to the bathroom but instead met with her assigned counselor during the 40-minute absence from class. The student was observed missing a portion of class at another time to do the same thing.

In a separate course on a different occasion, Cristina approached her instructor and explained that she was not feeling well. She explained further—"I am on my cycle" and needed to be excused from class. The instructor appropriately advised the student that she would need to be excused by her assigned counselor. Frustrated at the instructor's reply, Cristina immediately returned to her seat.

Cristina appeared to have difficulty grasping relevant course content in physiology. For example, during lectures, she would interrupt the instructor and comment that she was confused. When an attempt was made to help her better understand the lecture material, she took exception to examples used to help illustrate concepts or processes.

In her biochemistry class, Cristina emailed the course director several questions at a time, several times a day, and late into the night. Cristina appeared to understand the material but lacked confidence in her abilities or was focused on superfluous details. Cristina thought the instructor was extremely nice and a very good teacher.

In embryology, the instructor did not answer all of Cristina's questions but directed her to where she could find the information in the textbook and course notes. The instructor did not respond to her or any student emails after 5 p.m. During class, the instructor redirected Cristina to the main points of discussion. The instructor was the first to report back to the program director that Cristina thought her English skills were not good enough to comprehend concepts in the course.

The instructor disagreed. The instructor felt Cristina's behavior was manipulative and a distraction to the rest of the class.

Midway through the first semester, Cristina went to the program director and asked for an English tutor. When asked why she felt a tutor was needed, she said, "My English is not that good." Cristina was referred to the learning specialist for further assistance. The learning specialist wanted to know the exact nature of the English support, but Cristina was nonspecific. Not sure where to get a tutor at this point in the semester and how to get to the real issue, the learning specialist assigned a Hispanic mentor to the student.

When pressed for more details, Cristina began to list things that she "never knew" before, like the difference between *would, could,* and *should* or *neither* and *either.* Not sure of how to sensitively respond to the student's request for a tutor, the learning specialist said she would get back to her and reassured the student that she was up to the task.

The learning specialist reframed Cristina's educational experience to date. The completion of a high school diploma in the United States followed by the completion of a college degree in the United States had been accomplished. Neither one of these feats could have been accomplished without a significant command of the English language. The learning specialist told Cristina that "you would not have been admitted to a public university or this program without knowing how to speak, read, and write English." The learning specialist brought to Cristina's attention that her behavior heightened around exam time. She was showing classic signs of anxiety that was getting the best of her.

Prior to the start of the program, Cristina completed all of her medical school prerequisites at a community college. She got As in all her course work. She was shocked and in disbelief when she got a B- on the first quiz in embryology. She knew she studied hard but could not understand why she still did not get an A.

She was having a hard time understanding how the other students were getting better grades than her. Postbaccalaureate work was more challenging, and she was not prepared to deal with lower marks. The learning specialist advised her not to compare herself to other students and cautioned that improvement in courses often takes time to accomplish.

The learning specialist noticed a pattern with Cristina. A week before an exam or quiz, Cristina came into her office whining and complaining that "no one ever told me" or "no one is helping me." Cristina seemed to want to provide a rationale for her less than stellar performance before the exam was even given.

During the first semester, a faculty member and the janitor approached the program director about Cristina's complaining that no one was helping her. A meeting was set with the counselor and learning specialist together, as her story differed depending on who she was talking to. The student had a number of complaints, from health issues, to car problems, to household repairs. The counselor and the learning specialist used the session to allow the student to get all issues on the table so that they could be addressed.

Cristina's complaints of health issues and headaches had not been addressed for two years. The student had fears that her health concerns were more than she could handle, while at the same time she did not have enough time to take care of personal business. She did not want to seek medical treatment for a number of reasons, including losing her spot in the certificate program.

The learning specialist summarized her list of complaints and helped her develop a plan to get everything addressed in a timely manner. She was able to reframe the realities of time as a finite resource and to plan accordingly (time management is a theme throughout the program and was covered by both the learning specialist and the personal counselor). The counselor talked with the student about anxiety and how it needed to be under control. He made a referral to Counseling and Psychological Services (CAPS), a university resource. The student only needed to follow up as a result of this recommendation. The concern was that she could not continue with her current behavior, as she would wear out colleagues and staff with emotional and mental fatigue.

The student found additional counseling services on her own but had not followed up with the CAPS referral. The course work that continued through the second semester was a combination of self-directed learning, group learning, and small-group tutoring. Cristina made additional requests for tutors in both math and English. Through a series of dropping by the office, Cristina and the learning specialist missed each other. In dire need, Cristina asked the program director for help. The program director redirected her to the learning specialist. A few days passed, and Cristina did not respond to the learning specialist's emails.

After the third email, Cristina responded that she found someone on the main campus to help her, but she provided no other details. Once the learning specialist caught up to Cristina during a monthly meeting, the story had changed. She got help from an upperclassman in the medical school, but she could not remember the student's name who helped her. She was nonspecific about the type of assistance provided.

Another faculty member reached out to the program director to discuss Cristina's conduct in class. She was distracted by irrelevant facts. Specifically, the picayune nature of her questions was labor intensive and distracting to her peers. While not naming her specifically, one of her peers disclosed to the counselor that he or she was concerned about her well-being. She lashed out in class screaming and slamming books days before another exam. Some of her peers avoided studying with her because she was an energy drain, asking irrelevant questions.

The second semester concluded with monthly meetings with the learning specialist. Cristina did not report any problems or concerns. Occasionally she showed some insight to her behavior, crediting the learning specialist, counselor, or program director for bringing it to her attention. She ended each session with a note of gratitude for the certificate program and gave out hugs to the program staff.

FRAMING THE PROBLEM

Cristina is a 34-year-old female born in the southern United States to undocumented parents. She attended a public high school in a large urban city that had a significant Hispanic population. Cristina completed college in five years at a public state university with a dual-degree in communications and sociology. She completed her medical school prerequisites while working and paying her own tuition at a community college. She did well by earning all As. Cristina presents as affable and friendly, with an appearance that is always polished with makeup and stylish clothing. She successfully worked on the East Coast for 10 years for a bilingual marketing firm before deciding to change careers.

Career changers battle multiple emotions during their transition. A lack of confidence in a new discipline coupled with a sense of urgency for completion frame the dynamics. Cristina's inability to understand how her peers received better grades than her may be a direct indicator of the competitive nature that a career changer experiences from being at entry level again after several years of success in the chosen prior career. Redirecting the student to her transferable skills can serve to increase her confidence to continue.

To be a good doctor, she first needs to be a good patient. If she is indeed in pain or distress, she is required to take care of herself first. Everything suffers if she is not healthy. The technical standards requirement for the first year of medical school was explained. The program staff reiterated their belief in her ability to succeed to ease the multiple manifestations of anxiety displayed.

As one of two Hispanic students in the program, Cristina did not always gel with her classmates. Her professional experience as a bilingual account representative should have better prepared her for the interpersonal skills necessary in group dynamics.

DISCUSSION QUESTIONS

1. How did sharing her complaints with multiple parties (the counselor, learning specialist, janitor, classmates, and others) satiate Cristina?
2. Why did her story change based on who she was talking to? What was this indicative of?
3. What is one possible reason for the student not following up with the recommendations for assistance?
4. What were the student's core needs? Why did she not report problems or concerns at the close of the second semester?
5. How did neglecting her health for two years amplify her anxiety as a career changer?

Editors' Note: *This case is based on real student-professor interactions, but the names have been changed to protect the identities of those involved.*

SIX

"Where Do I Fit?"

International and Indigenous Students in Institutional Diversity Discourses

Eleni Oikonomidoy

On this particular date, a campus-wide committee continues the discussion about issues of diversity on campus. Administrative faculty, academic faculty, and a few students comprise the committee. Out of the approximately 15 regular members (there are many more who indicated an interest in the committee but do not show up to all meetings), there is one person from the office of international students who tirelessly brings up "international diversity perspectives" to the discussion.

The responses from the rest of the committee vary from enthusiastic (albeit temporal) agreements to absolute avoidance of the issues brought up. A similar dynamic exists with the representatives of the indigenous students on campus. When indigenous committee members are able to show up, their "voices" are somewhat included. However, when they are absent, they become invisible automatically.

Despite efforts to be recognized as an integral part of the diversity efforts on campus, international and indigenous students do not see themselves in the diversity discourse. This reality is further exacerbated by the physical and social distance that exists between the office that aims to assist international students with their social and academic integration and the office that focuses on the social and academic integration of diverse students on campus (from a student's perspective, the "diverse students" are perceived as those who are African American and/or Latino and perhaps those who are first generation to go to college). Indigenous students feel somewhat excluded from both places, despite efforts to create a subsection of the office for them. Some say that it is their numbers that make them feel invisible.

On this particular day, committee members, guided by the initiative of the chair of the committee, discuss the meaning of diversity on campus. Luckily, there is a person from the international office (Isabella) and an advisor for the indigenous students (Dena). At this particular moment, three committee members exchange their thoughts, with the rest of the members being bystanders. The three members are the committee chair (Tom), who brought the issue up and declared his keen interest in trying to understand others' thoughts; Isabella; and Dena. Here is an excerpt of their exchange:

Tom: Let's continue our discussion on the same topic for a minute, since not everyone has had an opportunity to participate. Let's hear from those who have not had a chance to talk at this time.

Isabella: OK, I sense that you are looking at me, so I will go first. I really fear that on this campus, international students are not really part of the diversity discourse.

Tom: But I feel that our committee has done a lot to try to include all students . . .

Isabella: I do not disagree with that statement. But given that I meet with international students every day, please allow me to share their views with you and the group. International students feel quite marginalized on campus. There seems to be an assumption that, because they are here for a certain period of time and their main goal is to study, they don't have to fully integrate to life on campus and in the United States. When efforts are implemented to sensitize faculty and administrators to the various needs and views of our student body through panels, movies, and so forth, international students are rarely included.

Furthermore, they feel excluded from the curriculum (Maramba, 2008). Finally, they are quite aware that their dedicated space (the office that aims to assist them) has very limited resources. While they do appreciate its existence, they long for opportunities to interact with their mentors for longer periods of time and for opportunities to mingle with other groups of students on campus.

Dena: If I may follow up on the points that Isabella brought up, I would like to offer similar observations from the perspective of the indigenous students on campus. All the issues discussed above are pertinent to them as well. An additional barrier that they face is their low numbers. Because we do not have huge numbers of indigenous students enrolled (we could of course contemplate the reasons why this may be), they tend to be invisible in the curriculum, in teaching, and in the campus-wide diversity efforts. Stereotypes and wrong perceptions block their attempts to engage with their peers. As a result, they withdraw to their own group.

Tom: I hear you . . .

Dena: Yes, because I am here today. If I were not here, then this point would have been mute. Those of us who are in small numbers do not have the luxury to be present in all meetings. I would like to challenge the committee to consider the implications of the points that Isabella and I brought up. It is not enough for our students to be included in mission statements and definitions of diversity. We would like them to have an equal presence in the day-to-day life on campus.

Isabella: Thank you, Dena, for raising these excellent points. I agree. Although the background experiences of our populations may be vastly different, they do share a common invisibility from the diversity discourse on campus. I hope that this can be addressed soon.

FRAMING THE PROBLEM

The committee heard the viewpoints of the representatives of two rather invisible groups of students on campus for the first time. Many members did not realize that the committee (among other bodies on campus) was inadvertently leaving groups of students behind. The issues that Dena and Isabella brought up provided food for thought. How many more groups of students did not have a "voice" in the supposedly inclusive committee because they did not have a seat at the table? The chair of the committee acknowledged the points that the two speakers had brought up. He thanked them both and invited all participants to think about the following and bring their thoughts to the next meeting. He then adjourned the meeting.

This meeting raises two important questions:

1. Was the committee's indirect message of inclusion of all students sufficient for people to feel included?
2. What could be done in order to ensure that there are no groups of students overlooked on campus?

DISCUSSION QUESTIONS

1. Did you find the points that Isabella and Dena made valid? Have you observed similar dynamics on your campus?
2. Is the active inclusion of all students possible within the current diversity discourses?
3. Do you perceive that there may be unconscious internal competition between various groups of students on campus?

4. How can spaces of inclusion for diverse groups of students refrain from becoming spaces of segregation? Who is/should be responsible for campus-wide efforts to build bridges?
5. What would be future steps for the committee to continue to engage in open dialogue about issues of inclusion in diversity in both academic and social spaces (Lake & Rittschof, 2012)?

Editors' Note: *This case study is a hypothetical scenario that represents real-world situations on college campuses across the nation.*

REFERENCES

Lake, R., & Rittschof, K. (2012). Looking deeper than the gradebook: Assessing cultural diversity attitudes among undergraduates. *Journal of the Scholarship of Teaching and Learning, 12*(3), 142–64.

Maramba, D. C. (2008). Immigrant families and the college experience: Perspectives of Filipina Americans. *Journal of College Student Development, 49*(4), 336–50.

SEVEN

Is Academic Advising Really Multicultural?

Doris W. Carroll

The foundation of college student success rests in the ability of a student to receive efficient, meaningful, and timely academic advising throughout their college years. Today, colleges are asking questions about the role and purpose of academic advising across the campus, across all majors and academic disciplines.

Academic advising is at the heart of student success.

That's all well and good, but it might be too late for James Bright, as he is about to leave school in disgust and frustration. The 28-year-old African-American male is frustrated because he cannot enroll in his last general education course that he needs to finish his bachelor of science degree in psychology.

James is an army military veteran who returned to State University (SU) two years ago after two tours of duty in Iraq and Afghanistan. He has been enrolled at SU for three semesters, having earned an associate's degree in psychology from Distance Global University (DGU), an institution that holds classes on the nearby army base.

James walked in to see his psychology advisor, Roberta Glower, and sat down in her office. Roberta glanced at her computer to review James's advising history. Without hesitation, Roberta proceeded to explain loudly:

James, you should have taken this biology class when you first arrived on campus. Don't you follow directions? I sent you an email about it last semester. You are gonna have to wait until next fall to enroll in it now. That course is over-enrolled, and I cannot add you to the class. What were you thinking? You have messed up. You're gonna have to push back your graduation date

31

one semester so that you can take this biology class. I'm not sure how I can help you now.

James replied,

Ma'am, I'm very sorry that I missed your email during that time, but I was hospitalized briefly during that semester for a recurring medical issue that was a result of my deployment. I missed some activities, and I was slow to return to class. I shared this information with the Veterans Affairs staff person within student services, and I just assumed that he sent that information to you. I would still like your help in getting into that biology class so that I might complete my degree on time this coming spring.

Roberta admitted that she was distracted in the advising session with James. When asked by a colleague, she acknowledged that she was preoccupied during her meeting with him, but she did not feel obliged to apologize to James for either her distractions nor her abrupt communication.

The Psychology Department has enjoyed a 5% growth in their undergraduate admissions. While this enrollment growth is seen as positive by the Arts and Sciences dean, the department will not receive any new academic advising support. So, for Roberta and her advising peers, it means additional work to support this new enrollment. Roberta is frustrated and overworked.

FRAMING THE PROBLEM

Academic advising can be viewed as a set of learning processes in which the student learner and the professional advisor join in transformational engagements. Multicultural academic advising involves several intentional activities that, when viewed together, provide support, respect, and recognition for students like James Bright. It is a cultural developmental process that assists students in the clarification of life or career goals and supports the development of educational plans. Additionally, multicultural advising involves clarifying that personal, career, and academic goals take place in a multicultural learning environment. This type of advising is heavily influenced and shaped by sociocultural, socioracial, and sociopolitical aspects of the campus environment.

Advising relationships involve culturally diverse individuals whose roles as advisees and advisors are multicultural in nature and context. The academic advising relationship between James and his advisor, Roberta, is most definitely a multicultural relationship. James is an African-American male and a military veteran. These are intersecting cultural identities that Roberta should understand and value when working with James.

It's unclear how she recognizes James's intersecting cultural identities in this short advising exchange. And yet, for James to receive effective and meaningful academic advising, it is important for Roberta to recognize and respect James's intersecting identities. Roberta is distracted, by her own admission, and these distractions make it difficult for her to understand these cultural influences within the academic advising interactions.

Effective multicultural advising includes a culturally based decision-making process that blends cultural, educational, and sociopolitical elements for the purpose of making meaningful educational and career decisions on behalf of the advisee. Lastly, multicultural advising is a cultural communication process and information exchange.

DISCUSSION QUESTIONS

1. What else should Roberta do to help James enroll in the spring semester biology class? Should Roberta apologize to James for her abruptness and insensitivity?
2. What are the cultural elements present in this advising interaction with James? How would you communicate the importance of these cultural elements to Roberta?
3. What additional campus resources would be helpful to James as he works to complete his degree?
4. What are the cultural advising skills that are important for Roberta to show or demonstrate in order to be a successful advisor for James?
5. What feedback should Roberta give to her supervisor about feeling overloaded? What additional professional development training would be helpful for Roberta?

Editors' Note: This case is one that the author created, and it represents an aggregate of experiences coming from her career in academe.

REFERENCE

Carroll, D. (2014). What is multicultural advising? In *Multicultural advising ebook*. Manhattan, KS: Kansas State University.

EIGHT

Nontraditional Students

Why Am I Here? Starting College at 25

Errick D. Farmer, Antoine Lovell, and Adriel A. Hilton

After graduating from high school at 17, Lance decided to go straight to work in the retail industry. Within two years, he was married, and together with his wife, they had a son. After working over seven years in a very demanding job, and a divorce, Lance decided it was time to consider something different.

After a few conversations with his brother, who at the time was finishing up a degree, he decided, why not? Lance decided to leave his full-time retail job, find a part-time job, and enroll full time as a student at a local community college.

At 25, Lance would set foot in his first college classroom. He was both excited and anxiously nervous about what he was about to encounter. As he settled into his first class and looked around the class of young 17- to 19-year-old students, he said to himself, "Why am I here?"

It was obvious that he was ready for the challenge and rigors of college-level work, but after being out of school so long, he questioned himself on how prepared he was. At this time, he realized he was a nontraditional student.

The National Center for Education Statistics (2011) defines nontraditional students as meeting one of seven characteristics: delayed enrollment into postsecondary education, attends college part-time, works full time, is financially independent for financial aid purposes, has dependents other than a spouse, is a single parent, or does not have a high school diploma. Those criteria fit a wide number of today's college students.

More than 47% of students who are enrolled in colleges and universities in the United States are older than 25 (Pelletier, 2010). However, for the context of this discussion, the age one begins actual pursuit of higher education is important.

According to the criteria above, Lance would meet five to six of the seven requirements. However, the real area of debate is that he is a new college student who is 25 years of age, and this is his first time in college. Lance certainly does not meet the requirement of a traditional student.

As a 25-year-old freshman, Lance certainly faced some challenges. Many of them involved how to navigate as a student around campus. When issues arrived, he did not fully know where to go and what resources were available to him. He often came to the conclusion that because he was an older student, many professors assumed he knew the answers.

As a full-time student, he felt like a fish out of water. Since he had been out of school for so long, he certainly had to catch up to many of the techniques being employed within the classroom. Adult students bring a different expectation to the teaching and learning experience. The teaching methods employed by instructors may not be the best method for adult learners who have been away from the classroom.

As Lance progressed through college, he definitely had his share of ups and downs. While the community college experience was very fruitful, he had a few setbacks. He failed a few courses and even had to withdraw from a few so he would not fail. He considered joining clubs and organizations; however, since it had been so long between a structured learning environment and because of his age, he did not fit socially. These items made it extremely difficult for him to be involved socially and academically. It was the sheer shame or embarrassment of asking a "colleague" for assistance who was at least seven to eight years younger than him. As an older adult, he felt he should be providing the assistance and not the other way around.

Fortunately, there is a good outcome to this story. Lance graduated from the community college, went on to a major university, and graduated with his bachelor's degree. He learned how to navigate through the community college and university processes and became an advocate for those true nontraditional students who seek higher education. Lance had the right mindset to find solutions. He is forever grateful for the experiences, but he often wonders if those in his situation are saying the same, "Why am I here?"

FRAMING THE PROBLEM

Lance is a new 25-year-old freshman who has never been in college before. Although he is ready, he's not sure he is up for the challenge. Yes, Lance had some challenges and ultimately persisted to graduation; however, as a true nontraditional student, what could have been done differently to assist Lance in this new and somewhat strange setting?

DISCUSSION QUESTIONS

1. Based on the current definition of a nontraditional student, do you think it is necessary to change the definition for this type of student?
2. What student resources could have been provided to Lance that could allow for a more seamless integration into college life?
3. Is it the responsibility of the college/university or each student to locate resources to assist in their progression through college? What would those resources be?
4. Lance felt embarrassed to seek help from his colleagues as a result of his age; how would you have dealt with his situation?
5. According to the National Center for Education Statistics (2011), nontraditional students have significantly lower retention and graduation rates when compared to their traditional counterparts. What barriers to degree completion could be recognized that would positively impact this trend?
6. Nontraditional students have different perspectives on social life (Greek life, sports, clubs) while in college. How might involvement in these activities enhance the learning experience for Lance?
7. As an older student, what implications should faculty consider in course design or what techniques should be employed in the class-room for course delivery?

Editors' Note: *This hypothetical situation represents a real-world problem in academe.*

REFERENCES

National Center for Education Statistics. (2011). *Projections of education statistics to 2019.* Retrieved from http://nces.ed.gov/pubs2011/2011017.pdf

Pelletier, S. G. (2010, Fall). Success for adult students. *Public Purpose,* 1–6. Retrieved May 10, 2017, from http://www.aascu.org/uploadedFiles/AASCU/Content/Root/MediaAndPublications/PublicPurposeMagazines/Issue/10fall_adult students.pdf

NINE

Empowering Women in Higher Education and Beyond

Kyung Hee Kim and Sean Schofield

Throughout history, cultural norms have promoted the idea that females are inferior to males. Girls and boys are born with similar potential, but traditionally, not all girls were either encouraged or supported to fulfill their potential (Kim, 2016). They were taught from their earliest years that they were less able to fulfill tasks and overcome challenges than males were. Cultural norms generated and reinforced by society, parents, and teachers have an oppressive influence on females, diminishing creativity and self-determination. Even when females represent a majority of the college population across America today, gender discrimination dominates campus climates.

Both scholarship and organizational leadership on campus are male dominated, with fewer females holding the highest-ranking staff positions, producing publications, and holding tenured faculty positions (West, Jacquet, King, Correll, & Bergstrom, 2013). Female students, especially those who return to school or pursue advanced degrees, face challenges beyond their male peers, perceiving higher familial pressure and lower institutional support (Stimpson & Filer, 2011).

Although the construct of femininity is comfortable to many people, it frequently diminishes females' uniqueness and career success, instead encouraging conformity to more compliant, less successful versions of themselves. Today's media have the capacity to empower women; however, they perpetuate gender inequality by silencing women's voices, ideas, experiences, and accomplishments. When working with colleagues or collaborators, some media acknowledge females' contributions and prominence less than males', devaluing the achievements of even the

37

most accomplished females (Kim, 2016). Gender inequality, although mitigated by laws and social criticism, still pervades through less apparent forms of prejudice like microaggressions.

Males outnumber females in senior positions with formal power, authority, high status, and high income, and females earn less than males, even with comparable levels of educational attainment and in similar industries and functions (U.S. Department of Labor, 2014). Progress in females' career development is not only negatively influenced by social barriers experienced from birth, but also from a lack of successful female role models in many industries.

APPLYING THE CATS FRAMEWORK

The Climates, Attitudes, Thinking skills (CATs) framework identifies the three steps that lead to individuals' success: first, cultivate the *climates* for success; second, nurture the *attitudes* that successful individuals exhibit in common; and third, apply *thinking* skills to achieve success (Kim, 2016). Sun, storm, soil, and space climates are the key to successful gardening. Similarly, the same four climates are essential for individuals' successful attitudes, regardless of their inborn potential: inspire and encourage them (like bright sun), set high expectations and challenge them (like fierce storms), provide them with diverse resources, experiences, and viewpoints (like diverse elements in soil), and provide them with the freedom to think deeply and differently (like free space and time).

THE BRIGHT SUN CLIMATE: INSPIRE AND
ENCOURAGE FEMALES TO VISUALIZE SUCCESS

The presence of female role models who can inspire and encourage females to persist in their academic and career choices is as critical to growth as the bright sun is to gardening. The high-paying science, technology, engineering, and mathematics (STEM) fields are traditionally male dominated. The lack of female role models prevents females from entering these fields, inhibiting career advancement. Females, from a very young age, must be introduced to heroines from whom they can draw inspiration and begin to visualize their future success (Austin & Nauta, 2015).

A lack of female role models inhibits the advancement of women within research areas, and in their recognition for global advancement. Most Nobel laureates had role models who were previous Nobel laureates, but with the small number of females historically awarded the Nobel Prize, few females have Nobel laureate role models or mentorship opportunities.

So they have less chance to win a Nobel Prize (Kim, 2016). To cultivate the sun climate, several universities have memberships with national women's mentorship organizations, like the Forte Foundation, which increase access to successful females and opportunities for collegiate women to witness the impact that women have on national and international scales.

THE FIERCE STORM CLIMATE: CHALLENGE FEMALES WITH HIGH EXPECTATIONS TO REACH THEIR POTENTIAL

For the storm climate, fostering females' strengths while providing appropriate support mechanisms and challenges is critical. The University of Illinois–Urbana-Champaign partners campus offices with community organizations to promote females' self-worth and self-advocacy. Northeastern University implements females' empowerment workshops through an active LinkedIn group, connecting students with females already in the workforce. These females can candidly discuss their experiences, demystify expectations, and establish relationships that can foster self-esteem and better equip them to persevere through challenges they may face during their transition from college to career.

Creating female career advancement opportunities is an important goal of many universities; however, universities must also focus on empowering students and communities to combat issues like sexual violence and sexual aggression that female students face at levels disproportionally higher than their males peers (National Sexual Violence Resource Center, 2015). Promoting a safe, inclusive, and nondiscriminatory environment is one of the chief responsibilities of every university.

Educating females and allies on recognizing potential perpetrator behaviors, which is risk-reduction education, is more effective than conventional, risk-aversion education. This shifts the traditional onus of safety from each woman's need to protect herself to calling upon the entire community to create a safe space for females (Foubert, Langhinrichsen-Rohling, Brasfield, & Hill, 2010). Some universities have adopted programs that focus on empowering females through increasing their sexual health knowledge, developing healthier attitudes and social norms, and educating bystanders to create communities of action.

THE DIVERSE SOIL CLIMATE: PROVIDE FEMALES WITH DIVERSE RESOURCES, MENTORS, AND VIEWPOINTS

For the soil climate, providing females with more resources and opportunities is critical. Some universities have developed programs designed to empower women through increasing self-image and creating a culture of support for women. The University of California–Davis, who prides themselves on being first in the nation for launching women into STEM careers, dedicates resources to females' advancement in the STEM fields and provides females with mentorship, funding, and research opportunities. Texas A&M University implements the American Association of University Women's salary negotiation workshops as a method to combat the wage gap.

Successful programs encourage women to think positively about their worth and futures by first introducing them to strategies for connecting with different people and exploring new viewpoints and potential directions and, second, empowering female students to utilize those strategies to develop a lifelong network that will continue to generate opportunities in the future (Kim, 2016).

THE FREE SPACE CLIMATE: FOSTER AND CELEBRATE FEMALES' UNIQUE IDENTITIES

For the free space climate, nurturing females' gender-bias-free attitude, rejecting gender stereotypes, and removing limitations to gender expressions, which ubiquitously surround campus every day, is critical. Nonconforming to conventional gender-role expectations and norms and resisting rigid gender-role expectations helps increase flexibility and adaptability in females, which enables a variety of thinking strategies and techniques beyond those prescribed for females.

Female students must view and use nonconformity as a strength by accessing and learning from both males and females. They must express both traditionally masculine attitudes (e.g., independence, confidence, assertiveness, and outspokenness) and feminine attitudes (e.g., softness and sensitivity) and characteristics. They must pursue their dreams regardless of gender, because even subtle gender-based limitations impact self-image. They must question the organizational norms that have been in place since a time when economic realities, social norms, and females' roles were different than they are today.

FRAMING THE PROBLEM

Shandra, a fictitious but representative student, is a bright, ambitious first-year scholar of color at a predominantly White university. She demonstrated strong academic ability while completing her first semester but feels isolated, unsupported, and detached from the university. She struggles to connect with peers, faculty, and staff members. She thinks that the Women's Center is primarily for women who are survivors of intimate partner or sexual violence. The student organizations on campus seem as foreign to her as her experience in her residence hall. She plans on transferring to a community college close to home, where she can feel at home again.

DISCUSSION QUESTIONS

1. Whose responsibility is it to ensure Shandra feels connected to and supported by the university?
2. What offices or programs could best assist Shandra as she explores and establishes her own sense of identity?
3. What systems on campus failed Shandra, and what improvements may have prevented her from falling "through the cracks?"
4. What larger issues might Shandra's leaving be indicative of?
5. What steps could be made to correct these issues?

REFERENCES

Austin, M. J., & Nauta, M. M. (2015). Entrepreneurial role-model exposure, self-efficacy, and women's entrepreneurial intentions. *Journal of Career Development, 43*, 260–72.

Foubert, J. D., Langhinrichsen-Rohling, J., Brasfield, H., & Hill, B. (2010). Effects of a rape awareness program on college women: Increasing bystander efficacy and willingness to intervene. *Journal of Community Psychology, 38*, 813–27.

Kim, K. H. (2016). *The creativity challenge: How we can recapture American innovation.* Amherst, NY: Prometheus.

National Sexual Violence Resource Center. (2015). *Statistics about sexual violence* [Data file]. Retrieved from https://www.nsvrc.org/sites/default/files/publications_nsvrc_factsheet_media-packet_statistics-about-sexual-violence_0.pdf

Stimpson, R. L., & Filer, K. L. (2011). Female graduate students' work-life balance and the student affairs professional. In P. A. Pasque & S. E. Nicholson (Eds.), *Empowering women in higher education and student affairs: Theory, research, narratives and practice from feminist perspectives* (pp. 69–84). Sterling, VA: Stylus.

U.S. Department of Labor. (2014). *Women's Bureau Data & Statistics: Earnings* [Graph illustration 2014 women's to men's earnings ratio and wage gap 2014]. Retrieved from https://www.dol.gov/wb/stats/earnings_2014.htm#Ratios

West, J. D., Jacquet, J., King, M. M., Correll, S. J., & Bergstrom, C. T. (2013). The role of gender in scholarly authorship. *PLoS One, 8*(7).

TEN

Thinking Differently Builds Passion on Campus

Kyung Hee Kim and Sue Hyeon Paek

Innovations are the unique and useful outcomes of the multiyear process of creativity. Creativity begins with the spark of curiosity and interest. This spark can be fanned through memorization, comprehension, and application into the flame of mastery, a deep knowledge and set of skills, such as know-how or expertise. The process that turns curiosities and interests into a passion is called inbox thinking. This passion is not found overnight; it is developed over a period of years. Without the hard work of inbox thinking, even students with great creative potential may only become frustrated dreamers who never develop their true passion.

If students rely only on inbox thinking, lacking fluent, flexible, and original outbox imagination, experts may simply become boring technicians. Instead, they can identify a problem in their chosen area through a playful imagination, further fueling their passion. Outbox thinking should be followed to generate distinctive ideas and potential solutions to solve the problem beyond the convention in the area. Then students must test the solutions by analyzing and evaluating their usefulness through deep-inbox thinking, which is called critical thinking (Kim, 2016).

Students begin to combine solutions that they have selected and then refine them by working on the details while pursuing simplicity, which is called newbox connections. Newbox connections contribute to an innovation that benefits themselves and others, which fulfill their purpose in life. This is why developing students' inbox, outbox, and newbox (ION) thinking should be the ultimate goal of universities. Through supporting ION thinking, universities can play major roles in leading innovation and economic development, as exemplified by Silicon Valley, which has flourished by means of ION thinking skills fostered by Stanford University in the technology industry (Kim, 2016).

Uniqueness, in addition to usefulness, is necessary for innovation. However, as the U.S. education system has become increasingly obsessed with testing and focused on rote learning since the 1990s, students have learned to refrain from thinking differently and generating exceptional ideas (Kim, 2016). In fact, the more students are eager to succeed in school, the more they conform to standards and rules to avoid possible failures, instead of pursuing the risky road of innovation. For instance, students avoid doing writing assignments without templates and detailed examples, inhibiting themselves from free thinking and eventually resulting in lack of diverse or novel ideas on campus. Further, test-centric education fosters competition instead of collaboration by ranking students against each other so that they are reluctant to share ideas and blend efforts.

Even students with high scores in an academic subject are often not interested in learning more about it because they lack opportunities to apply what they have learned into real-world situations, viewing an examination or grade as a terminal point, rather than applying their knowledge to the world. Instead of just doing what school tells them to do, students interested in living their own purposes should consider these four major steps (Kim, 2016):

I.   Find their curiosities and interests.
II. Develop them into their passion.
III. Expand outbox imagination for the passion.
IV. Build newbox connections for the passion.

STEP I: HOW TO FIND CURIOSITIES AND INTERESTS

1. Look Outside School

Test-centric education lets students fall into a routine that leaves them bored or unfulfilled, and they know neither what they are interested in nor what else they can do. If they look outside school, they would be likely to find more opportunities tapping into their motivations or lighting their curiosities. This separates them from others and sets them on the path of unlocking who they are. It will also cut down on in-school competition and provide more options for success.

If they want to find diverse opportunities outside school, they might ask themselves:

- What extracurricular activities have attracted me?
- Where can I find resources outside of school to further my understanding of these activities or introduce me to new potential curiosities and interests?

2. *Separate Passion from Financial Gain*

From an early age, children learn that a passion must be related to money. If they are drawn to a subject area that deviates from traditionally high-paying industries, parents frequently say things like, "You cannot make a living from doing that." After a long time of doing what others expect of them, college students often ask in a hopeless way, "How can I find my passion?" This really means, "How can I get paid for doing something I enjoy?" However, if they wish to spend their life doing something they love, they should abandon their financial concerns (for now) and ask themselves:

- What would I spend every day doing if money were of no concern?
- What could I do for five years even without getting paid?

3. *Find What You Spend Time On*

Often, students who feel lost in their search for purpose have interests that they are not even aware of. The things they naturally do without conscious pursuit are clues about where they excel or what they enjoy. If they examine the topics or activities that dominate their free time, conversations, and web browsing, they might find their hidden interests. They can identify things they usually do by asking themselves:

- What activity am I immersed in when I lose track of the time?
- What activity do I hate stopping?

They can also counterargue to find what they love to by asking themselves:

- Do I do this because I want to please someone else?
- What do I dislike doing?

4. *Identify What Comes Easily to You*

What students do in their everyday life with ease is likely connected to what they are interested in doing. They can identify the tasks that friends or family ask them to do as a favor. These favors are likely what they do with ease, even if they do not recognize it themselves. They can identify the big and little things that come naturally to them and build on their strengths by asking themselves:

- What is something that I can teach others to do?
- What types of things do close friends or family usually seek my input on?

If students cannot find one thing they can do with ease, they might find several things they can do with some effort. They can combine these things together and develop them into something far greater. Here are some questions they can ask themselves:

- What has been common feedback on what I am good or not bad at?
- What are my best experiences in my life, and what do they have in common?

5. Find What You Enjoyed Doing in the Past

When college students were younger, many of them had big dreams and were open to all possibilities about what they could do or become. Returning to that dreamy, possibly unrealistic attitude again, bringing out their childlike wonder and their playful adventure, will help them find their interests. They can remember things, activities, and interests from childhood before others started telling them what to do by asking themselves:

- What activities bring me back to my childhood?
- What (e.g., games, books, habits) did I enjoy before I thought about the judgments of others?
- What dreams have I given up on?

Additionally, they can identify the circumstances they successfully moved through in the past, which enables a perspective that others do not have. This helps them identify their strengths, build on them, and use them to help others who have a similar journey by asking themselves:

- What is the hardest thing I have ever overcome? How did it impact me?
- What time or place have I felt most alive?

STEP II: HOW TO DEVELOP A PASSION

Experience Mastery Feelings

Many confuse greatly liking something with feeling passionate about it; however, true passion comes with time, effort, and mastery. When students feel they have begun to master something, their excitement rises, which makes them come back for more. This ensures they concentrate their efforts on the most rewarding things, thereby improving their skills and enhancing their strengths.

Set and Remember the Goals

Students can find and emulate role models by (a) listing people they respect or envy, (b) learning about their work and how and why they were able to remain successful, and (c) setting small and big goals. When setting goals, they must break patterns of nonproductive thinking by replacing self-dialogue like "I am not sure I can" with "I can do this." They can identify what they want to avoid followed by eliminating negative statements and set their goals using positive statements and specifically defining what they do want.

As it is easy for students to lose track of big goals in the web of their daily obligations, they should actively and mindfully track their progress. They should find ways to incorporate their big goals into their everyday activities and make time to take small steps. They can grow their awareness by finding collaborators or mentors who can hold them accountable and work alongside them. They can also use reminders of their big goal such as notes, images, and inspirations that reinforce their goal or excite them in down moments.

STEP III: HOW TO EXPAND OUTBOX IMAGINATION FOR THE PASSION

Exceptionally successful people in history were obsessed with solving a problem or improving something in their field. Students can find a problem by asking what has frustrated them. A problem does not have to be big. Simply finding one little thing a day to be curious about or interested in can lead students to their next big goals. Once they identify a problem, they must generate as many solutions as possible to solve the problem. Until achieving a certain number of solutions, they should avoid judging their solutions to encourage the free flow of their thoughts. They can develop solutions by challenging themselves every day, such as experimenting with or exploring new activities or possibilities, and overcoming the fear of making mistakes, rejection, or failure.

STEP IV: HOW TO BUILD NEWBOX CONNECTIONS

After testing the practicality of those solutions, students can select and combine the most unique and potentially useful ones. They can combine the strengths and expertise of themselves and others in unique and useful ways. They can restructure and build a synthesis of those selected solutions and then improve and reinterpret the synthesized one through the refining process of working on details and pursuing simplicity. If they continuously elaborate details without pursuing simplicity, it would become more remarkable but too complicated to be useful or be completed. Unessential elements should be eliminated through repeatedly elaborating and trimming over a long period.

FRAMING THE PROBLEM

Brian, a fictitious student who represents many real students, has participated in the university honors program since his first year. His GPA has never dropped below 3.5, which he is very proud of and is eager to maintain. He always thinks about what professors expect of him and follows rubrics and examples for assignments. Brian never thinks about what he wants or what topic or subject interests him. Sometimes interesting ideas appear in his mind, but he never uses them for his assignments and just follows professors' directions.

DISCUSSION QUESTIONS

1. What anxiety or fears do you think Brian might have if he were asked to approach homework differently? More creatively?
2. In what ways do you recommend he use his own ideas?
3. What institutionalized or individual supports might help him think about what he wants to do with his life?
4. What type of student could Brian become if he were to build newbox connections?
5. How could Brian's professors expect more from him? How could they get him to truly think critically?
6. Do you think Brian could ever see that critical thinking is more important than GPA in terms of real life and his future?

REFERENCE

Kim, K. H. (2016). *The creativity challenge: How we can recapture American innovation.* Amherst, NY: Prometheus.

ELEVEN

Redefining Mentorships

Strategies for First-Generation College Students' Success

Kyung Hee Kim and Nancy Chae

Campus diversity may include race, gender, intellect, language, socio-economic status, and other forms, and first-generation college students (FGCSs). FGCSs are first in their families to attend college, and they represent about a quarter of enrolled college students in the United States (Redford & Hoyer, 2017). Although FGCSs increasingly enter colleges, they are a marginalized minority group on campus, and universities should be committed to supporting FGCSs' completion of their bachelor's degree, which is critical to become competitive and succeed in the workforce.

FGCSs tend to demonstrate great resilience, a hard-work ethic, academic motivation, and social engagement on campus (e.g., Demetriou, Meece, Eaker-Rich, & Powell, 2017; Longwell-Grice, Adsitt, Mullins, & Serrata, 2016). However, they may also experience financial, academic, and social inequities on campus: (a) financially, more FGCSs come from lower-income families, take out loans, and have one or more jobs while in school compared to other students, increasing their dropout rate due to financial burden (Redford & Hoyer, 2017); (b) academically, fewer FGCSs enroll in highly selective colleges than other students, feel less confident about their abilities, and demonstrate lower levels of college readiness (Redford & Hoyer, 2017); and (c) socially or culturally, more FGCSs feel marginalized, reporting experiencing racism, classism, and low expectations from faculty and not seeking supports compared to other students (Martin, 2015).

To increase FGCSs' access to, or knowledge of, financial, academic, and social resources on campus, mentorships can bridge a gap to help minority students, including FGCSs, successfully navigate their academic and social experiences on campus and improve their communication skills, academic achievements, and degree completions (e.g., Demetriou et al., 2017; Longwell-Grice et al., 2016; Martin, 2015). The research-based CATs model (Kim, 2016) identifies three steps for individuals' success: first, cultivate the *climates* for success; second, nurture the *attitudes* that successful individuals exhibit in common; and third, foster *thinking skills* to achieve success.

This model can be applied to successful mentorships for FGCSs. Like climates that are essential to successful gardening, the sun, storm, soil, and space (4S) climates are the keys to promoting and highlighting FGCSs' successful attitudes. Although on-campus organizations may assign mentors to mentees, mentees must earn mentors through their mentored attitude, which is one of the most critical attitudes that all exceptionally successful individuals exhibit (Kim, 2016). This chapter first discusses how mentorships cultivate the 4S climates for FGCS; and second, it addresses how FGCSs can develop the mentored attitude to seek, establish, and maintain a meaningful mentoring relationship while enhancing their thinking skills.

MENTORSHIP CULTIVATES THE 4S CLIMATES

Mentorship focuses on both personal and professional development, where mentors are trusted role models for mentees. Mentors share their expertise, provide mentees with intellectual and psychological support, and advance mentees' knowledge and skills through constructive feedback. Bright sun, fierce storms, diverse soil, and free space (4S) climates are necessary for mentees to flourish, and mentorships cultivate the 4S climates (Kim, 2016):

1. Like the bright sun that gives plants warmth and light to grow well and upward, mentors inspire FGCSs to pursue big ideas and encourage them to follow their curiosities by:

   - Being and identifying role models whom FGCSs admire or aspire to pursue their achievements, skills, and attitudes.
   - Exposing FGCSs to future possibilities and encouraging playful thinking and questioning.
   - Supporting FGCSs to build on existing knowledge and fill in gaps.

2. Like fierce storms that provide water for plants and help plants grow strong, mentors set high expectations for and challenge mentees with brutally honest feedback by:

- Being impartial and providing constructive criticism.
- Nurturing FGCSs' self-efficacy on specific strengths while treating them as equals.
- Empowering FGCSs through challenging experiences to build resiliency.

3. Like diverse elements in the soil that help plants to grow healthy, mentors provide mentees with enriching and diverse resources, experiences, and viewpoints, instead of giving the right answer to a problem by:

- Teaching FGCSs to be resourceful and access tools for their learning and growth.
- Promoting FGCSs' values and career goals yet providing them with alternative perspectives.
- Nurturing FGCSs' open-mindedness by exposing them to new experiences and opportunities.
- Networking FGCSs with collaborators within their area of interest.

4. Like free space that allows plants to grow to their maximum potential, mentors provide mentees with the emotional space and time to think deeply and behave differently by:

- Providing space and time for FGCSs to absorb new information, enjoy deep thoughts in solitude, and develop their own ideas for a problem before collaborating with others.
- Encouraging mentees to take intellectual risks and discover and use their uniqueness to achieve their goals.

MENTEES DEVELOP THE MENTORED ATTITUDE

Mentors know how to leverage resources to support mentees and value their investment of time to help those who are willing to help themselves. FGCSs must develop their mentored attitude and practice to get noticed by potential mentors (Kim, 2016) by:

- Sharing their values, challenges, aspirations, and favorite subjects.
- Demonstrating their drive to continue growing through learning and reading.
- Sharing their visions in concise and compelling ways and committing to achieve their visions.
- Sharing short- and long-term goals and seeking skills and experiences to pursue the goals.
- Promoting others' success and practicing self-disclosure.

Mentors and mentees develop trust over time by mentees first asking for guidance, not mentorship, from mentors and maintaining flexible and professional relationships. After establishing trust, FGCSs may seek an introduction or introduce themselves to potential mentors. FGCSs must research role models whom they can aspire to become, discover what potential mentors can offer, and delineate how mentors can help them. Mentorships must be built on mutually beneficial relationships in which both the mentees and the mentors get the most out of the relationship. FGCSs must try to add value greater than the time that mentors spend on them before expecting anything in return (Kim, 2016), and FGCSs can:

- Offer knowledge, skills, or resources to benefit mentors and assist with projects or tasks.
- Make the mentorship experience enjoyable and bring humor to challenges.
- Be good listeners and approach mentors' advice with enthusiastic interest.
- Act on mentors' advice and modify FGCS's beliefs, instead of seeking confirmations of what they already believe.
- Use time with mentors wisely by asking questions that cannot be easily found and be prepared for meetings.
- Bring solutions, not just questions; seek perspectives, not only answers; and use mentors' perspectives to map their next steps.
- Follow up and follow through with commitments and share mentorship results and impacts.
- Master knowledge and skills, yet remain teachable by continuously evaluating themselves.

Friends may tell friends what they want to hear, but mentors tell mentees what they need to hear. FGCSs must shift their perspectives by appreciating and learning from, rather than becoming offended or disappointed by, constructive feedback. FGCSs must try to recognize mentors' care and investment in the mentorship relationship and seek feedback to continue their growth. FGCSs must try to appreciate mentors' brutally honest feedback (Kim, 2016) by:

- Being open and humble about the gaps between their own knowledge and mentors' and demonstrating their willingness to be taught.
- Viewing mistakes as opportunities to learn and grow by soliciting mentors' specific feedback and asking questions about how to improve for the challenges ahead.
- Encouraging mentors to push FGCSs to try new things and test new ideas and increasing FGCSs' self-efficacy by exploring their interests beyond their comfort zone.

Mentorships are meaningful relationships, not charitable acts. FGCSs must try to show appreciation, gratitude, generosity, and loyalty to mentors (Kim, 2016) by:

- Going the extra mile to show their:
    - o gratitude both verbally and through actions, such as thoughtfully writing thank-you notes or emails.
    - o continued growth by updating mentors with their progress.
    - o dedication to maintain their partnership over time, instead of contacting mentors only when they need help.

- Sharing or recommending resources, articles, books, posts, or other information that might be interesting or useful to mentors, which saves the mentors' time in searching for such information.
- Updating mentors with newfound insights in their subject matter.
- Working diligently on topics important to the mentors, requesting more responsibilities, and contributing in expansive ways.
- Connecting FGCSs' research interests with their mentors' ongoing interests.
- Publicly crediting who and what got them there, and paying it forward by encouraging future mentees with the same value and attention that their own mentors had given them.

Mentors and mentees grow from each other's ideas and enthusiasm, as well as recognize, support, and celebrate each other's achievements. Mentorships must ensure healthy and thriving relationships by welcoming disagreements, which revitalize mentors' productivity and develop FGCSs' critical-thinking skills. FGCSs must not only take but also give feedback to mentors and disagree with them (Kim, 2016) by:

- Challenging mentors and voicing their opinions respectfully, not defensively.
- Offering constructive feedback on mentors' projects and providing suggestions for improvement.
- Discussing and debating ideas, which provide both mentors and FGCSs with new perspectives and sharpen their critical-thinking skills.

FRAMING THE PROBLEM

Brian (who is a fictitious but representative student) is the first in his family to attend college. He has worked diligently to balance his academic course load and work-study job on campus. Brian is double majoring in psychology and music. The resident advisor (RA) knew about Brian's academic interests and mentioned a male psychology professor, Dr. Smith, who taught upper-level cognitive psychology courses.

Brian did not know much about cognition and was not an upperclassman yet, so he sought advice from his RA about how to prepare for his initial meeting with Dr. Smith. The RA recommended that Brian briefly read and prepare questions about cognition. Brian scheduled a visit to Dr. Smith's office during his office hour.

Dr. Smith welcomed the conversation and personally and professionally connected with Brian's transition to college as a first-generation college student. Brian felt comfortable and was inspired by Dr. Smith, and likewise, Dr. Smith appreciated Brian's curious nature and felt that he demonstrated much potential. Dr. Smith encouraged Brian to share new insights in their following meeting, and as a result, Brian did more than just research on cognition and found fascinating studies about music and cognitive development, connecting his passions together.

DISCUSSION QUESTIONS

1. In what ways did Brian demonstrate the mentored attitude?
2. How did Dr. Smith cultivate Brian's 4S climates, and what additional ways can he continue to cultivate Brian's 4S climates?
3. What are ways to promote mentored attitude in FGCSs?
4. What forms of mentorship programs are available on your campus? To what extent are these programs supportive of FGCSs' needs?
5. What support systems and individuals are and are not available on your campus to support the needs of FGCSs? What professional development are needed to prepare various support systems and individuals on campus to connect FGCSs with potential mentors and provide meaningful mentorship opportunities?

REFERENCES

Demetriou, C., Meece, J., Eaker-Rich, D., & Powell, C. (2017). The activities, roles, and relationships of successful first-generation college students. *Journal of College Student Development, 58,* 19–36.

Kim, K. H. (2016). *The creativity challenge: How we can recapture American innovation.* Amherst, NY: Prometheus.

Longwell-Grice, R., Adsitt, N. Z., Mullins, K., & Serrata, W. (2016). The first ones: Three studies on first-generation students. *NACADA Journal, 36*(2), 34–46.

Martin, J. P. (2015). The invisible hand of social capital: Narratives of first generation college students in engineering. *International Journal of Engineering Education, 31,* 1170–81.

Redford, J., & Hoyer, K. M. (2017). *First-generation and continuing-generation college
   students: A comparison of high school and post-secondary experiences.* Retrieved from
   the National Center for Education Statistics: Institute of Education Sciences
   website: https://nces.ed.gov/pubs2018/2018009.pdf

UNIT 2
CLASSROOM CLIMATE

TWELVE

Diversity and Classroom Instruction

Managing Difficult Discussions

Tamara Zellars Buck

On August 17, 20-year-old Anthony Chappell was shot and killed by a police officer as he ran away from where he was standing with three other men of similar age, height, and build outside a convenience store in a large midwestern city.

The officer mistakenly believed Chappell had snatched the purse of an elderly woman in the downtown shopping district earlier in the day and sought to arrest him. Four hours after the shooting, it was revealed Chappell was not the suspect and had no criminal record.

Chappell was an African American.

As the story was breaking, local news anchor Don Pennington referred to Chappell as "one of many thugs who has been plaguing our city" during crosstalk with another news anchor. Pennington's comments became a national part of the story after the NAACP and the National Association of Black Journalists protested and called for his termination.

On August 21, the news anchor was suspended for six weeks.

The shooting took place about 75 miles from Eastern State University, a four-year regional state institution. About 40% of all ESU students hailed from the city, and another 15% lived within 100 miles of the city. Roughly 8% of ESU's student population is African American.

ESU has a department of mass communications that serves 526 majors who are pursuing an undergraduate degree in one of three major concentrations: broadcasting, digital journalism, and public relations. Mass communications majors must earn 120 credit hours to graduate, including a minimum of 40 credit hours in mass communication courses and a minimum of 72 credit hours earned outside of the department.

All mass communications majors must take a combination of required and elective courses in their concentration that total at least 21 credit hours, plus an additional seven core curriculum courses totaling 19 credit hours.

One of the core courses is Media Diversity, a course that examines the portrayals, perceptions, and challenges of minorities in mass media content and media professions. The department offered two 30-seat sections of Media Diversity in the semester that the shooting occurred. Professors Judy Miller and Kathy McDonald, both fourth-year instructors within the department, were assigned to teach the sections.

Miller, who is 33 years old, is a dark-skinned African-American journalism professor who lived and worked for 10 years in Atlanta, Georgia, before joining the ESU faculty. She has taught Media Diversity four times previously and is known for making students feel safe when they express opinions, even unpopular ones, in the course.

Miller has generally been a well-liked professor by students. Most former students say she has an assertive personality and is an entertaining lecturer who likes controversy. She relies heavily on real-life examples and modern scenarios to demonstrate concepts in the course.

"I loved Media Diversity because I could tell the truth, and I knew she would, too," wrote one student on www.whatsmyprofessorlike. com. "It got deep in there sometimes, but she [Miller] always knew how to handle it."

Comments received from her detractors are in line with one student's claim that "She race baits a lot. Everything can't be blamed on White men, even if they are the primary ones in power," and another student's comment that "I don't think we have a diversity problem anymore. That stuff is in the past."

This will be McDonald's first semester teaching Media Diversity. She is a 55-year-old broadcast professor who worked in Tulsa, Oklahoma, television news for 20 years before joining the faculty. She was born and raised in Argentina and is considered a White Latin American. She has as much teaching experience as Miller but is considered to have a more comforting, laid-back personality.

"She's helpful and easygoing," a student wrote on www.whatmyprofessorlike.com. "She's a very chill teacher, and I've never seen her mad or upset." Negative comments about McDonald that appeared on the website said she was "OK but read from the textbook a lot." One student wrote that he wondered "if she ever actually watched the news, because she never talks about it."

In June, Miller had offered to meet with McDonald to discuss classroom management strategies after learning that McDonald would be teaching Media Diversity for the first time.

"You'll have a mix of students from urban and rural areas, and when you start talking about things like race and sexuality, you are going to hear some offensive opinions," Miller told McDonald. "Are you ready for what might happen next in your classroom?"

McDonald declined Miller's offer of help because she thought their teaching strategies would not mesh well.

"I'm going to stick to the book and take a more theoretical and historical approach to the materials," McDonald said. "I think I can contain things better this way."

ESU students were aware of the Chappell shooting and the anchor's remarks, and it was a leading topic as they returned to campus in the fall. On the first day of her Media Diversity class, Miller played a video clip of the breaking news story and subsequent statements by the anchor. She told her students the anchor's remarks applied perfectly to the course, and they would follow the story throughout the semester and discuss it whenever it was relevant.

Ann, a White female who had been raised in a nondiverse rural community near the university, raised her hand.

"I'm always hearing about crime statistics in the city, and it always looks like it's a Black man—I mean an African American—who is involved," she said. "I can understand why the anchor talked about thugs."

"But the problem is Anthony Chappell wasn't a thug," Lionel, who is also White and sat in the row behind Ann, snapped. "He [the news anchor] just made a racist statement and should have been fired. Your kind of racist thinking is why we have a problem now."

Miller saw Ann sink into her seat and casually positioned herself between the two students as she responded.

"Wait, Lionel," Miller said. "Let's focus on the issues and not start name-calling."

Miller explained how news media persistently overrepresent African-American men in crime stories, and how that misrepresentation can impact people's perceptions about criminal behavior over time.

"The media has created this stereotype that has influenced how many of us look at Black men and other minority groups," Miller said. "Ann's perceptions are actually very natural under the circumstances. What we want to do is recognize what's happening so we can learn to look at and perceive information differently. That's how we change things in our industry."

After these statements, both students seemed to relax, and Lionel even apologized to Ann. After class, Ann walked up to Miller and gave an apology of her own. "I didn't mean to offend you," she said. "I haven't been around a lot of different people, and I'm just used to the old way of doing things, I guess."

Miller told Ann she wasn't offended.

"This class is about teaching you how to do things better than we've done professionally in the past," she said. "I can't do that if you don't recognize that there's a problem, and I don't ever want you to be afraid to voice your opinion."

McDonald did not mention the Chappell shooting or the news anchor's remarks on the first day of class. After Pennington's suspension was announced in the second week of the semester, an African-American student named Ty Burrows brought it up in class.

Burrows lived in the city and had participated in protests against the television station before the semester began. McDonald told him she preferred not to talk about current events in the class and would rather focus on case studies provided in the textbook.

"That doesn't make sense," Burrows replied heatedly. "In that White man's eyes, I'm a thug, and it's like we deserve what we get or something. This is why people don't like the police or the media."

Before McDonald could reply, Andrea Dodge, a White student in the back of the room, spoke up.

"Why'd he run if he didn't do something wrong?" she asked. "He [the anchor] didn't mean all of you are thugs. He was just saying that innocent people don't run. We can't blame everything on the media."

The two students began to exchange angry remarks, and McDonald was unsure how to shut down the conversation. As other students in the class became visibly uncomfortable, she hurriedly spoke over them and dismissed the class 30 minutes early. McDonald then quickly left the room and returned to her office. After closing her office door, she wondered how she could have handled things differently.

FRAMING THE PROBLEM

Prior to the start of the semester at a regional state university, a young African-American male in a nearby city was shot by a police officer who mistakenly thought he was a suspect in a purse snatching who was evading arrest. The story drew national attention after a local news anchor referred to the victim as "one of many thugs who has been plaguing our city" during crosstalk with another news anchor.

Mass communication majors at the university are required to take a diversity course in which they discuss the portrayals, perceptions, and challenges of minorities in mass media content and media professions. Two sections of the course are being taught this semester, one by an African-American professor who has previously taught the course, and the other by a White Latin American professor who is teaching it for the first time.

The two have different personalities and classroom management styles and have not shared strategies for addressing conflicts that may arise in the classroom.

The veteran professor, who is comfortable using real-life scenarios in the classroom, chose to initiate discussion about the shooting and the news anchor's remarks from the first day of class. When a conservative student's opinion was aggressively rebuffed in class, the professor physically created a barrier between the two students and gently reprimanded the opposing student for name-calling. She used both students' viewpoints to explain how the situation related to the course work before returning to her lecture.

The novice professor, who chose a more theoretical and historical approach to teaching in order to contain potential controversy, was reluctant to discuss the situation during class. When a heated discussion arose between two students, she was unable to manage the conversation and ultimately canceled class a half hour early. She left the classroom before her students and returned to her office.

DISCUSSION QUESTIONS

1. What tactics did Miller use to control the classroom discussion? Why do you think they were effective?
2. How do you think Miller would have handled the situation that McDonald faced?
3. Can you think of any potential problems that might have resulted if McDonald had not canceled class when she did? What potential problems could she have caused by canceling class as she did?
4. Can you tell when professors are uncomfortable talking about race, sexuality, religion, gender identity, or similar subjects? How?
5. What are the benefits and problems that may result from discussing controversial current events related to diversity in the classroom?

Editors' Note: This case study represents a combination of real scenarios, but some of the details were changed to protect the identities of those involved.

THIRTEEN

Can Online Teaching Be Inclusive?

Doris W. Carroll

Professor Sam (Samantha) Jones was excited to begin teaching developmental psychology online to undergraduate psychology majors. She has fought long and hard for the creation of this new online course and was looking forward to teaching it during the spring semester.

Professor Jones designed her syllabus carefully and was committed to adding developmental models about special underrepresented populations. She created learning modules for each developmental model and assigned students as group leaders to lead each week's online discussion. She created a special learning module to explain the developmental process for gay, lesbian, bisexual, and questioning young adults and included recent research about this cohort of individuals.

Professor Jones's class had 25 distance undergraduate students, and each was assigned to one of four online groups.

Terri, a 32-year-old female, single-parent adult learner, was the Group 4 discussion leader for Week 6. As discussion group leader, her responsibility was to create and post discussion questions for her group members to begin their discussion on Tuesday.

During Week 5, Terri emails Professor Jones and complains about not being able to read the assignment reading materials for the upcoming Week 6. Terri has low vision, and she uses a read-aloud text software to help her read textbook assignments and other course documents. The PDF copy was scanned poorly, and the print is very light on the page, making it difficult for Terri's text-to-speech software to read the document properly. Moreover, it contained some highlighted text and headers that complicated the document's readability. Annoyed and frustrated,

Terri emails Professor Jones and complains to her about the poor quality of the reading assignment for next week.

Annoyed, Professor Jones responds to Terri by saying,

> Why are you just now telling me that you need an accommodation for my class? We are five weeks into the course. You should have said something to me early in the semester. I am not sure that I can help you now, since we are now in the middle of the class. Go see the Disability Support for Students Center to see if they can help you find another way to make this reading accessible to you. I can't figure it out.

Terri grumbles but manages to post her discussion questions, despite the fact that she could not read the documents very well. Terri posts two questions for Group 4. The first question asks, "Would you feel safe going into the gender-neutral bathroom? As a woman, a male in the bathroom stall next to me is very scary."

Her second question was equally insensitive: "Do you really believe in same-sex relationships?"

Terri did go visit with the Disability Support for Students Center, but she went there mainly to complain about Professor Jones's unwillingness to help her. Terri informs Mr. James White, the Disability Support for Students Center director, that Professor Jones was unwilling to help her and fussed at her because she was late in making her request for a disability accommodation.

Mr. White explains to Terri her eligibility for disability services and reviews the procedures for eligibility. Terri did ask for assistance in reading the PDF and other class text documents. Before she can receive the assistance, Terri must follow the registration process for receiving academic or transportation accommodations. In the coming days, Terri will need to provide a letter of documentation regarding her visual impairment from her physician.

The next day, Professor Jones emails Terri to express concern about the discussion questions she had posted in Group 4. Professor Jones points out that her discussion reflects an overt bias against transgender students and same-sex couples. She informs Terri that she has asked her group members how they felt about those discussion questions.

Two members were uncomfortable with the questions that Terri wrote, expressing their perceptions that such questions reflected a cultural bias against GLBTQ persons. The other group members were offended by the questions and did not agree with them. Professor Jones then asked Terri to amend or modify her questions:

> We want to promote an open learning climate in our distance class so that we can have honest and genuine conversations about the developmental aspects of GLTBQ identity. Your questions shut the conversation down in your group because they reflect only your attitudes and beliefs that are biased and narrow.

Terri snapped back, "No, I'm not gonna change my questions. They'll just have to deal with it. When it's their turn to be group leader, they'll see just how hard it is!"

FRAMING THE PROBLEM

Building an inclusive learning climate online involves several elements: instructional design of course materials, structural and organizational climate issues, and culture-specific content for the course. This case presents unavoidable intersecting cultural and inclusiveness issues.

First, there is the matter of inclusive access to the learning management systems and to all the course materials regardless of students' ability status. Professor Jones is challenged to make certain that the class online materials are open and available to Terri, as they are available to all other students in the class. Understanding that obligation and staying aware of the ways that new technologies can support online students with disabilities is an ongoing learning process for online teachers.

Second, Professor Jones has a responsibility to make certain that the online learning environment is safe for all students to offer comments and ask questions related to course materials and class discussions online. This responsibility means that the online instructor has the duty to make certain that class members engage one another in a respectful manner, in keeping with university policies regarding student conduct and behavior. Learning and student engagement must take place within a climate of openness, fairness, and respect so that everyone can participate in classroom learning fairly and equitably.

The discussion questions posted by Terri raise issues about their fairness and inclusiveness regarding the GLBTQ population. Professor Jones has an obligation to address the offensive nature of those questions to assure the learning environment remains open, fair, and inclusive for all students. Terri's discussion questions were offensive and disruptive to overall classroom learning, but she can learn how to engage her peers in ways that will promote open-minded, positive comments and new dialogue about GLBTQ developmental models.

DISCUSSION QUESTIONS

1. What would you say to Professor Jones about her comments and response to Terri's accommodation request? What additional actions should Professor Jones do to support Terri's accommodation request?

2. What is Mr. White permitted to say to Professor Jones about Terri's accommodation request? When can he share that information with Professor Jones, according to FERPA guidelines? Are there other federal guidelines that impact Mr. White's communication?
3. What must a student do to make an accommodation request to an instructor?
4. How might Professor Jones have handled the matter of Terri's biased group discussion questions? Should Terri's questions be removed or taken down? If so, then by whom?
5. What should Professor Jones say to the members of Terri's small group regarding the offensive discussion questions?
6. What other actions should Professor Jones do within her online class to make certain that all class members feel safe?

Editors' Note: *This case is one that the author created, and it represents an aggregate of experiences coming from her academic experiences in teaching online courses. It does not represent any one student, nor class.*

REFERENCE

Stavredes, Tina. (2011). *Effective online teaching: Foundations and strategies for student success.* San Francisco, CA: Jossey-Bass.

FOURTEEN

What Happens When No One Sees You for Who You Are?

Sherwood Thompson

Mary registered for a very popular course on campus, and she is elated when she is admitted. Mary arrives the first day of class on time and takes her seat on the front row. As she waits eagerly for Professor Watson to begin, she sits among other students—all White. Mary is Hispanic.

Right on time, Professor Watson opens the class with a short self-introduction, a brief overview of the course, an explanation of the syllabus, and a review of the required textbooks. He then asks his students to give a two-minute introduction that includes their hometown, their major, their reason for enrolling in his class, and one accomplishment that they are proud to share with others.

Mary is the third student to introduce herself. She follows the order of the introduction instructions, and before sharing the thing of which she is most proud, she takes a long pause and then confidently tells the class that she is gay. The introductions continue without delay, but she notices a repulsive glance from Professor Watson. The students are quiet, and the class progresses in a somber mood.

Professor Watson gave the following week's assignment, and class was over. Everyone walked out, but Mary was the last one to leave the classroom. She reflected on what she experienced: the silence, the professor's sharp glance, and the alienation of the other students. It all adds up to what she determines is potential prejudice toward her. Considering her status as a Hispanic gay female, she begins to understand this combination as unwelcome on her midwestern college campus.

Mary tried to remain upbeat about the class, but she felt hurt psychologically. On the other hand, she felt determined and strong enough to withstand the strange stares and the razor-sharp silence from her classmates. She decided to remain enrolled in Professor Watson's class regardless of the potential prejudice and discrimination she might face. She made up her mind to succeed in the course.

When she considered that first day in class again while walking to her residential hall, Mary had to laugh. She was surprised by the ways in which some people in the 21st century seem so out of touch with reality. She made up her mind then that she was going to organize a Gay-Straight Alliance (GSA). She felt that if she could help circulate more information about the gay lifestyle, then others might be more accepting of LBGTQ lifestyles and rights. Mary had many great, straight friends, and she believed that these friends would be willing to assist her in organizing the first GSA on campus.

Mary conducted some research that night before going to bed, and she found that larger universities had GSAs on campus. She discovered that the GSA is a valuable resource for LGBTQ students, helping them to deal positively with bullying and other forms of harassment. She drew up an organizational plan, a list of student friends, and finally located the student organization application form that was required to establish a recognized organization on her campus. Her next steps were to find a faculty advisor and 10 members.

FRAMING THE PROBLEM

Mary was eager to take Professor Watson's class because she had heard that he was a fun professor and very engaging in class. After introducing herself that first day, however, Mary was surprised to learn that the class regarded her gay identification as something "uncool." Both her classmates and the professor were unresponsive—even chilly—and Mary knew that she was the reason for the solemn attitudes moving forward. She felt uncomfortable.

Mary did not pity herself, though. Instead, she immediately decided to organize a GSA on campus with the purpose of educating fellow students and even faculty about issues of LGBTQ people. Her secondary purpose for organizing a campus GSA was to seek allies who might assist her in promoting cultural awareness on campus about the LGBTQ community.

DISCUSSION QUESTIONS

1. Based on her unexpected classroom experience, what thoughts do you think were going through Mary's head? Do you think she was

surprised, hurt, disappointed, or saddened; or was she ambivalent toward her classmates' behavior?

2. What attempts might Professor Watson have made to comfort Mary or show his understanding, despite his negative facial expression after Mary's announcement that she was gay?

3. Do you think that Mary will find supportive students willing to join the newly organized GSA organization? Will she find a supportive faculty advisor? Why or why not?

4. How can a person's sexuality be accepted and respected among straight people without treating LGBTQ individuals as if they are weird and impaired?

5. What are some ways of fostering a learning community that practices core values and beliefs that make all people feel welcome and comfortable on campus?

Editors' Note: This hypothetical scenario does not depict actual students or instructors, but rather it represents the type of interactions that can occur on campuses across the country.

FIFTEEN

Being an Ally

Learning to Listen before Trying to Advocate

Kirsten LaMantia and Holly Wagner

Professor Frankl had assigned an advocacy project to her class. The purpose of the project was for students to pick a marginalized population with whom they were unfamiliar, research it, interview a member of that population, and engage in some sort of advocacy for the population as a whole.

A couple weeks after introducing this assignment, Dr. Frankl asked the students which populations they were considering. One of the students, Jack, said, "I'm planning on learning more about Scientology." Dr. Frankl was puzzled and said, "How are Scientologists marginalized?" Jack replied, "Well, people look down on them sometimes."

Dr. Frankl asked the class what they thought. Some of the students explained why they did not think Scientology would work with this project, as they were not one of the groups they had learned about in class. Dr. Frankl then took time to reteach the class about systemic marginalization and oppression and explained that both are symptoms of a much larger problem about power and inequities.

Dr. Frankl then asked the class how they would be able to advocate for a population that was not marginalized or oppressed. The class answered that they did not know if it would be possible. Dr. Frankl explained that we can always work to create tolerance among different beliefs, cultures, ethnicities, and races, but that it would be difficult to advocate and become an ally for a privileged group.

Dr. Frankl explained to the class that in order to be an ally students must look for guidance from the group for which they would like to advocate. If someone with privilege and power chooses to do "good" for others without first truly understanding the lived experiences and needs of that marginalized group, then the person will be much more likely to do harm than good.

Dr. Frankl used a metaphor by saying, "I want you to be a megaphone rather than being the person using it. Meaning, as people with privilege, it is your job to listen to the stories of the marginalized and amplify those stories rather than making them about you."

She then pulled up Amélie Lamont's website *Guide to Allyship*, which further explained what it means to be an ally and advocate. The *Guide to Allyship* states that it is "an ever-evolving and growing open source guide meant to provide . . . resources for becoming a more effective ally." Dr. Frankl asked the class to take a break and read the website while thinking about the population for whom they would like to advocate to see if they were following the rules set forth by Lamont.

When the students came back from break, they told Dr. Frankl that they had a better understanding of what it meant to be an ally and that they were ready to discuss which populations they chose.

Dr. Frankl said, "It sounds like allyship is making more sense to you now, I'm glad to hear that! How might you take this knowledge and apply it to the next steps in this project?"

Jack raised his hand and said, "I think I might actually choose the African-American population. My mom is a cop, so I only hear her perspective on stuff like Black Lives Matter. Now I'm wondering if there's another side to the story."

A transgender student, Frankie, raised their hand and said, "I want to be a better ally for undocumented people. After reading this website, I think I might need to talk to my friend's parents who are undocumented and see what issues they face within our community."

Dr. Frankl emphasized Frankie's point and finished the discussion by saying, "Yes! In order to best understand how to advocate, we must have difficult conversations with those around us. We cannot build our ally muscles while remaining silent or ignoring our privilege. I am looking forward to hearing how you choose to advocate for marginalized populations."

FRAMING THE PROBLEM

Dr. Frankl is an associate professor at a midsize university. She teaches multicultural awareness and advocacy and is in the process of introducing the cumulative project for her course. Dr. Frankl allows her students to choose specific populations for whom to advocate and apply the process of becoming an ally. She begins each semester with explaining different levels of privilege such as White privilege, male privilege, and cisgender privilege.

Initially, this particular class was averse to accepting their individualized privileges and voiced their concerns. Dr. Frankl addressed these concerns before moving on to the selection of appropriate criteria for marginalized populations for whom to advocate. One student voices his thoughts about a population he would like to learn more about, yet this particular population was not marginalized, though it was not fully understood by many. The discussion that ensued highlights the propriety of which populations with whom we as allies choose to work.

DISCUSSION QUESTIONS

1. Do you agree with Dr. Frankl that it is difficult to advocate for and become an ally for a privileged group? Why or why not?
2. Does the fact that Jack believes Scientologists are looked down upon qualify them to be a group for which to advocate?
3. What was your reaction to Dr. Frankl's megaphone metaphor? Would you use this or something similar to portray advocacy and allyship? Why or why not?
4. In addition to Lamont's *Guide to Allyship*, what other resources could you share with your students to elicit the intricacies of becoming and being an ally?
5. What kinds of difficult conversations have you personally had with members of marginalized groups that may have helped you better understand and advocate for them?
6. How would you encourage your students to begin these difficult and courageous conversations?

Editors' Note: This case study represents the real experiences of a professor, but some of the details are a composite, and some have been changed slightly to protect the identity of the students.

REFERENCE

Lamont, A. (N.d.). *Guide to Allyship*. Retrieved December 1, 2017, from www.guidetoallyship.com

SIXTEEN

Code Switching

Double Consciousness in the Classroom

Antoine Lovell, Errick D. Farmer, and Adriel A. Hilton

Zion is a 21-year-old heterosexual male that subscribes to normative behaviors of masculinity. He was born and raised in the Cherry Hill section of Baltimore, Maryland, where according to the Baltimore City Health Department (2011), the median household income was $19,183 per year. Zion received his bachelor's degree in sociology from Howard University and is now pursuing a master's degree in social work at Columbia University School of Social Work.

He graduated from Howard University with a 3.8 GPA and was inducted into the Alpha Kappa Delta Honor Society—Sociology. Zion decided on Columbia because of its prestige and availability of resources. Particularly, Zion wants to utilize his acquired skills as a social worker to address mental health in African-American communities throughout Baltimore.

Men social workers are more likely to identify mental health as their primary area of practice (National Association of Social Workers: The Center for Workforce Studies, 2004). Zion's upbringing in a low-income household in Baltimore is quite different from the ivory towers of Columbia University, yet he is invested in social work scholarship and the university community. As an African-American male, Zion stands out from the mostly White, non-Hispanic female students.

According to the U.S. Department of Labor, Bureau of Labor Statistics (2017), African Americans make up a paltry 22.7% of the social work population. The combination of Zion's race/ethnicity and his 6'8", 220-pound frame is not what one thinks of as the ideal social worker. Ideally, the identity of a social worker is reflected in the demographics, whereas

81.5% of workforce participants are women (U.S. Department of Labor, Bureau of Labor Statistics, 2017).

Zion is passionate about social work and is frequently outspoken about clinical interventions in his classes at Columbia. As a learning opportunity for students, the professor asks that they each do role-plays of individual interventions. A scenario is presented to students, and they are to act them out in accordance with social work principles. Each assignment is worth 40% of the students' grade. The students are instructed to be empathic and soothing to their client, and to appear nurturing.

Bringing his whole self into the classroom, Zion approaches the clinical intervention by utilizing his Baltimore dialect that is representative of his culture and values—while incorporating social work techniques. The professor grades Zion on his clinical approach and gives him a grade of 20/40 for his role-play assignment. She notes that he was graded down for the assignment because he did not display empathy in his tone, nor did he appear nurturing enough to the client during the exchange.

Further, Zion was advised to watch his female colleagues and their verbal approach to working with clients and mimic their style in order to be successful in the program. The professor stated to Zion, "Urban vernacular is not appropriate in the classroom within an Ivy League setting, nor is it suitable for a clinical intervention with marginalized clients."

She further explained to him that as an African-American man who is educated, he should begin to speak proper English. He explained to the professor that his voice is naturally deep and that he cannot mimic his female colleague's tone. Additionally, Zion expressed frustration with the professor because he felt that she was whitewashing the exercise by not acknowledging his style in working with clients.

Zion's tone during the clinical intervention was reflective of his close identification with masculinity and is not closely associated with the traditional way of social work. The traditional way of experiencing and implementing social work practices is associated with women and nurturing behaviors.

Furness (2012) suggests that "male and female behaviors are shaped in that children are rewarded or punished for acting out roles and this is reinforced through their identification and membership of same-sex groups" (p. 484). In social work practice, "men can be seen as a potential threat, but also not possessing innate feminine characteristics associated with caring" (Furness, 2012, p. 485).

The history of social work practice, and the current gender imbalance within the discipline, marginalizes men in classrooms and the field. A close relationship with traditional social work ideology that is characterized by nurturing behavior is weighed heavily toward positive outcomes for women and may be in direct opposition against African-American men. Research shows that heterosexual African-American men endorse traditional masculinity (Abreu, Goodyear, Campos, & Newcomb, 2000; Levant, Majors, & Kelley, 1998).

Zion has to maintain a 3.5 GPA at Columbia University to maintain his scholarship. Because of his grade for the role-play, the highest grade he can achieve in the class is a B. He is frustrated because he does not have the ability to mimic a population that he has not had close contact with; it denies who he is, while stigmatizing the very community that he wishes to work with once he graduates. His language is what connects him to his community and is an important aspect of his identity.

FRAMING THE PROBLEM

In an ever-changing world with numerous ethnic and racial identities, the ability for educators to understand various forms of communication is critical to the success of students of color. Multiple ways of learning in the classroom, inclusive of various dialects and dialogue, is essential in acknowledging the personhood of each student, which carries culture and values in its delivery.

Code switching is a technique utilized by students to function in mainstream society, while holding on to the essence of their personhood. Code switching for students of color has become a survival technique in a world that legitimizes values and traditions that may not be reflective of their culture.

Particularly, the education system perpetuates traditions associated with White, non-Hispanic groups that are hired in classrooms that are disproportionately White (Gillborn, 2005; Leonardo, 2002). In 2016, 82% of teachers in the United States identified as White, non-Hispanic (U.S. Department of Education, 2016). For students of color, code switching is as essential to the academic experience as learning the alphabet is a measure of school readiness.

Code switching is a part of what W. E. B. Du Bois labeled as a double consciousness, whereas students of color are forced to transform and develop an alternate means of expression that deviates from their normal mode of communication (Brannon, Markus, & Taylor, 2015; Brown, 2009). The implementation of code-switching pedagogies in the classroom is essential in providing an equitable space that is inclusive of all cultures and encourages the deconstruction of traditional White normative behaviors. According to Hill (2009), "code-switching pedagogies call for employing students' home language to facilitate appropriate nonstandard and standard contexts for writing and speaking" (p. 121).

DISCUSSION QUESTIONS

1. Based on the current scenario, does Zion have an obligation to code-switch in order to improve the quality of services to his clients in the future?
2. What student resources could have been provided to Zion for him to be successful in the classroom?
3. Is it the responsibility of the professor to be culturally receptive, or does she have a responsibility to social work as a field?
4. What are some of the institutional barriers that are presented to Zion as he seeks a graduate degree in social work?
5. What code-switching pedagogies can be implemented for students like Zion to be successful?
6. What role does race and gender have in the dynamics described between Zion and his professor?
7. How could the professor acknowledge Zion's culture and values while upholding social work practices?

Editors' Note: *Zion is a hypothetical student who represents real issues that occur in higher education.*

REFERENCES

Abreu, J. M., Goodyear, R. K., Campos, A., & Newcomb, M. D. (2000). Ethnic belonging and traditional masculinity ideology among African Americans, European Americans, and Latinos. *Psychology of Men & Masculinity*, 75–86.

Anderson, M., Astin, A. W., Bell, D. A., Cole, J. B., Etzioni, A., Gellhorn, W., et al. (1993). Why the shortage of Black professors? *Journal of Blacks in Higher Education*, 25–34.

Baltimore City Health Department. (2011). *2011 neighborhood health profile Cherry Hill*. Baltimore, MD: Baltimore City Health Department.

Brannon, T. N., Markus, H. R., & Taylor, V. J. (2015). "Two souls, two thoughts," two self-schemas: Double consciousness can have positive academic consequences for African Americans. *Journal of Personality and Social Psychology*, *108*(4), 586–609.

Brown, A. L. (2009). "O brotha where art thou?" Examining the ideological discourses of African American male teachers working with African American male students. *Race Ethnicity and Education*, *12*(4), 473–93.

Furness, S. (2012). Gender at work: Characteristics of failing social work students. *British Journal of Social Work*, *42*, 480–99.

Gillborn, D. (2005). Education policy as an act of white supremacy: Whiteness, critical race theory and education reform. *Journal of Education Policy*, *20*, 485–505.

Hill, K. D. (2009). Code-switching pedagogies and African American student voices: Acceptance and resistance. *Journal of Adolescent & Adult Literacy* *53*(2), 120–31.

Leonardo, Z. (2002). The souls of white folk: Critical pedagogy, whiteness studies, and globalization discourse. *Race Ethnicity and Education, 5,* 29–50.

Levant, R. F., Majors, R. G., & Kelley, M. L. (1998). Masculinity ideology among young African American and European American women and men in different regions of the United States. *Cultural Diversity and Mental Health, 4*(3), 227–36.

National Association of Social Workers: The Center for Workforce Studies. (2004). *2004 national study of licensed social workers demographic fact sheet—male social workers.* Retrieved May 12, 2017, from National Association of Social Workers: The Center for Workforce Studies: http://workforce.socialworkers.org/stud ies/demo_fact_male.asp

National Association of Social Workers. (2008). *Social workers at work.* Washington, DC: National Association of Social Workers.

U.S. Department of Education. (2016, July). *The state of racial diversity in the educator workforce.* Retrieved May 8, 2017, from U.S. Department of Education: https:// www2.ed.gov/rschstat/eval/highered/racial-diversity/state-racial-diversity -workforce.pdf

U.S. Department of Labor, Bureau of Labor Statistics. (2017, February 8). *Labor force statistics from the current population survey.* Retrieved May 15, 2017, from https://www.bls.gov/cps/cpsaat11.htm

Whitaker, T., Weismiller, T., & Clark, E. (2006). *Assuring the sufficiency of a front-line workforce: A national study of licensed social workers, special report; Social work services in behavioral health care settings.* National Association of Social Workers, Washington, DC.

SEVENTEEN

A Faculty Member Protecting the Marginalized

Kathy Previs

"Michelle" is a transgender student who had recently been "Michael," a name he was given at birth. While Michelle did not undergo a sex-change operation, she self-identifies as a female. She is tall, thin, dresses stylishly, and wears makeup, much like many female students do. However, her voice is still deep, and her "Adam's apple" is noticeable. She attends a midsize public university located between the Southeast and Midwest regions of the United States.

Dr. Rice had been teaching public speaking for at least 10 years when he came to his course at the beginning of the fall semester where he met Michelle who sat in the center of the classroom. In his classroom over the years, he has heard and graded many speeches that ranged in a variety of topics. Having taught in both private and public colleges and universities, he has met and educated students from all walks of life. They have hailed from countries around the world, from a mix of socioeconomic and ethnic backgrounds with different cultural practices, and with a variety of political and religious beliefs.

One of the challenges of teaching public speaking, or any course that delves into controversial topics, is tempering emotions when students speak openly and passionately about topics for which they are attempting to persuade their audience into thinking as they do. To this end, the content of the subject matter is being addressed. But what happens when the speaker him- or herself is the subject of disagreement or controversy?

During Dr. Rice's first semester at this university that is located in a traditionally politically conservative state, Michelle took the podium to deliver her first speech. The audience seemed amused at her presence, more interested in the way she looked rather than what she would have to say. She was dressed in jeans and a colorful sweater, with hair perfectly coiffed and makeup applied carefully to accent her features. She appeared to be nervous as she began to speak, but yet there was also a visible determination to get through the speech. Both of these are traits of public-speaking students regardless of who they are or what their background is.

Once Michelle began to speak, Dr. Rice heard snickers from class members. He noticed several students in the classroom looking at one another, making faces, hiding laughter, and texting one another. He also saw several students who sat quietly, watching and listening to the speaker, just as they would any other speaker, with the utmost respect and politeness they were taught to exhibit during a speech.

As Michelle continued to talk, you could tell she was becoming more and more uncomfortable, and negative student reactions were not helping. At this point, Dr. Rice was faced with a decision: Should he immediately stop Michelle and remind the audience how to treat a speaker with respect, or should he let Michelle continue to deliver her speech and hope that the next four minutes pass by quickly? If he were to interrupt the speech, Dr. Rice would be treating Michelle differently than other speakers. After all, they were not interrupted despite having difficulty with the speech. If he did not interrupt Michelle, then it might appear that he condoned what the audience was doing, and clearly he did not.

According to research, faculty can do several things to make classrooms more inclusive. For example, Zane (2016) suggests the following ways to be in compliance with Title IX protections, which protects students and employees from sexual harassment but also protects individuals from harassment based on gender and gender identity, "including acts of verbal, nonverbal, or physical aggression, intimidation, or hostility based on sex or sex stereotyping, even if those acts do not involve conduct of a sexual nature" (Zane, 2016).

To support diversity, particularly in academic settings, Zane (2016) recommends the following strategies be implemented in the classroom:

1. Set the tone: Create guidelines in the syllabus and communicate them on the first day of class.
2. Model desired behavior.
3. Preserve confidentiality.
4. Adopt more inclusive language.

Let's apply Zane's (2016) recommendations above to Dr. Rice's situation. The first recommendation is setting the tone by creating guidelines in the syllabus and communicating them on the first day of class. Dr. Rice did this by including the following passage in his syllabus:

To encourage and achieve a positive learning environment, students are expected to display respect for classmates and instructor by avoiding racist, sexist, or other negative verbal or nonverbal messages that may make others in our classroom community uncomfortable. You must be willing to listen to others' opinions, even if they are different from your own. Part of being a good speaker is being a good (read: polite) listener. **Failure to abide by these rules will result in point deductions from *your* speech, NOT the student who is speaking.**

Dr. Rice read this statement to the class and asked if there were any questions about what constituted appropriate behavior. There were no questions when he read it during the first week of class.

For the second recommendation, Dr. Rice exhibited the behaviors described above, even for speeches for which he himself disagreed with the stance of the speaker. He did this by politely listening and asking appropriate questions, if he had any, that did not embarrass the student.

Third, though it did not apply to this particular situation, Dr. Rice has protected the confidentiality of students who have come to him with problems, or has sought individuals who could help them with interpersonal or legal problems if he was not able to help them.

The fourth recommendation is to adopt more inclusive language in class documents. Zane (2016) offers the following examples: use *partner* or *significant other* instead of *boyfriend/girlfriend* or *husband/wife*; avoid titles such as *Mr., Mrs.,* and *Ms.*; instead of calling the class *guys*, use *everyone, you all,* or *you.* Dr. Rice practices these suggestions whenever the opportunities present themselves.

While scholars can offer suggestions in how to create the optimal learning environment, many faculty are often faced with dilemmas to which authors have not yet offered solutions. Although Dr. Rice implemented several strategies to create a comfortable classroom environment that supported diversity, he found himself caught in the middle of a situation that would either help or hinder the student.

Rather than cut Michelle off while students were making fun of her, instead, he allowed her to finish her speech and then let the next few students deliver their speeches. At the end of the class period, he reread the passage from the syllabus (included above) and reminded students that several had lost points on their speeches for displaying offensive nonverbal behaviors. This way he did not single Michelle out among the other students.

FRAMING THE PROBLEM

It is imperative that diverse students be protected. However, at what point does protecting students who are different become "special treatment"? In stepping in to protect a student, the mere stepping in might draw increased attention to an already sensitive situation. In the situation described above, based on an actual experience at a university, the professor was faced with the dilemma of stopping students from harassing another student, while being mindful not to embarrass or call additional attention to the student.

DISCUSSION QUESTIONS

1. Do you think Dr. Rice properly handled the situation when he noticed students were bullying Michelle? What, if anything, would you have done differently?
2. What do you think might have happened if the professor stopped Michelle in the middle of her speech and reprimanded the students making fun of Michelle? Do you think it would have made matters worse or better?
3. Do you believe that Michelle's classmates had a responsibility, along with the professor, of stopping students from making fun of Michelle?
4. Can you think of a situation on your college campus where a student, because he or she is different from those who are in the majority, encountered bullying in some form? How did the professor handle it?
5. Based on your experiences in college, what other dilemmas have faculty faced in terms of handling diverse students?
6. In your opinion, how can students help faculty to identify forms of bullying or other forms of marginalization that he or she might not recognize in his or her own classroom?
7. Are there additional recommendations you would add to Zane's (2016) list?

Editors' Note: This is an actual situation that occurred on a college campus. The names of the professor, student, and university have been changed to protect their identities.

REFERENCE

Zane, S. (2016). *Supporting transgender students in the classroom.* Retrieved from https://www.facultyfocus.com/articles/effective-classroom-management/supporting-transgender-students-classroom/

EIGHTEEN

LGBTQ+ Populations

Exploring Gender and Sexual Identities

Kirsten LaMantia and Holly Wagner

Dr. Jones was asked to guest lecture to an undergraduate class about creating LGBTQ+ inclusive environments within the students' future workplaces. She prepared a visual presentation that encompassed LGBTQ+ populations and the people within them. Her plan was to quickly go over the queer umbrella and then use a majority of the presentation to explore ways in which students were already working toward inclusive environments within their workplaces.

She began the presentation by asking the students if there is anything they feared about the topic of LGBTQ+ people, any specific questions they had, and anything they hoped to learn from the presentation. To her surprise, one of the students raised her hand and said that she did not know what LGBTQ stood for. Some of the other students in the classroom echoed her question.

Dr. Jones then realized that her presentation would already be too advanced based on where this class placed on understanding anything other than heterosexual couples.

First, Dr. Jones talked to the class about how she did not expect the students to change their values based on this presentation. Instead, she wanted them to be willing to learn about LGBTQ+ folks so that they could begin to better understand how to work with diverse clients in the future.

"I know your beliefs are important to you. We can't ask you to change them. And I know something that is really important to you is to help others and make the world a better place. Part of that means being able to help anyone who comes your way, regardless of your values. The more open you are to learning about this today, the better help you will be in your career. Not to mention, the more inclusive your workplace is, the more business you might be able to have."

Dr. Jones went through each letter and explained what *lesbian, gay, bisexual, transgender, queer, questioning, intersex,* and *asexual* meant. Before each definition, she asked the class if they had any idea about the definition of the letter. As she continued speaking with the class, she allowed them to ask more questions. She made sure to return any question from one student back to the whole class in hopes of creating an active dialogue, rather than a one-sided call and answer.

Dr. Jones then pulled up a collage of internet celebrities and actors who identified as LGBTQ+, such as Janet Mock and Portia de Rossi. She explained that though we might have a picture in our heads of what it means to be under the LGBTQ+ umbrella, all people are different, and just because you have heard the story of one person does not mean you have heard the story of all people. She also explained that intersectionality (the concept that marginalized groups have commonality) is important when talking about LGBTQ+ peoples and that race and ethnicity can play a huge role in the experience of a person under this umbrella.

At this point she asked the class members if they had any comments.

A student named Jaden, who sat toward the middle of the room, raised his hand and said, "Everyone in here knows I'm biracial. We've talked about it a little bit. But something I haven't shared is that I'm also bisexual. It's been really hard for me because I feel like I don't fit in with anyone. I'm always stuck in the middle."

Dr. Jones observed the reactions of the class and saw one of Jaden's classmates put her hand on his shoulder. Dr. Jones allowed a pause, and during that time, Jaden's peer said, "It means so much to me that you said this Jaden."

Dr. Jones ended the discussion by saying, "We may never know who identifies as LGBTQ+, and if we work to learn more about these communities and challenging our own biases, we might end up creating inclusive workplaces after all."

FRAMING THE PROBLEM

Dr. Jones is an openly gay, tenured faculty member at a smaller urban university. Her colleague is untenured and expresses discomfort with bringing up controversial topics. Dr. Jones is accustomed to broaching difficult topics surrounding racism, sexism, and other issues regarding oppression and inequality within her classes. She often facilitates dialogue among students to bring about awareness and insight into these issues, while gently challenging students to learn more about various perspectives from a more culturally competent framework.

Dr. Jones has prepared a presentation on LGBTQQIA populations for an undergraduate class yet is not certain from what level of awareness and insight these students are operating. Therefore, she brings in materials but is also prepared to assess the needs of the class and base the progression of her class presentation and discussion on those needs.

DISCUSSION QUESTIONS

1. What do you think about Dr. Jones's statement to the class regarding not wanting to change their beliefs and values, but instead asking them to be open to learning about different background and identities in order to be helpful? Do you agree or disagree?
2. What other examples or resources would you have used to help students relate to the various LGBTQQIA populations?
3. How might you augment Dr. Jones's introduction to the topic of intersectionality as applied to working with LGBTQQIA populations?
4. What was your reaction to Jaden's disclosure? How would you have handled his comments and his willingness to be vulnerable with his classmates?

Editors' Note: This case study represents the real experiences of a professor, but some of the details are a composite, and some have been changed slightly to protect the identity of the students.

NINETEEN

I'm NOT Chinese; I'm Japanese!

A Case Study of Stereotypes

Mustapha Jourdini

The United States continues to be an attractive study-abroad destination to millions of international students interested in pursuing quality higher education and research opportunities overseas. According to the 2017 Open Doors report, there were 1,078,822 international students in the United States. These same students added more than $39 billion to the American economy in 2016 (Open Doors, 2017). Notably, the majority of these international students came from Asia, led by China (32.5%), India (17.3%), and South Korea (5.4%) (Institute of International Education, 2017).

Beyond their positive economic impact on the U.S. economy, international students also have an educational and cultural impact on American students and faculty (Jourdini, 2014). Indeed, sharing their rich cultures with a university community on a regular basis will likely increase dialogue and enhance understanding of different world cultures.

While culture has been defined in a variety of ways, cultural identity is understood to subsume racial and ethnic characteristics. The shared spaces, values, beliefs, customs, and thinking patterns common to a particular group of citizens help shape an individual's cultural identity. Therefore, mistaking an international student's cultural identity, a source of pride and distinction, can sometimes be a costly and unforgivable sin.

Cultural identity is arguably the most important trait an individual holds dear and will fight, if not die, for when breached. One of the common stereotypes about Asians, which offends them greatly, is when a curious observer confuses their looks with the origin of their home country. Such confusion is all too common among students and educators alike.

Take, for instance, the following hypothetical class scenario from a college campus that prides itself on celebrating diversity and inclusion.

Jessica Walberg, a sophomore communications major, innocently makes an offensive comment about Akiko Matsumoto, a Japanese student at a U.S. university, seeking an undergraduate degree in interior design. While looking Akiko in the eye during a class discussion about health and wellness, Jessica blurted out, "Yeah, in China where you're from, pollution is horrible. The Communist government there is corrupt and is not doing much to curb environmental pollution."

Jessica's comment made Akiko confused and offended. With a flushing face, Akiko almost stiflingly whispered, "I'm not Chinese. I'm Japanese."

To make matters worse, Jessica added hurriedly, "That's correct; Japan is famous for Pokémon. My bad!"

Jessica's correction is supposed to be simultaneously a compliment and an apology to the Japanese culture and people for calling them Chinese. The course professor, Kelly Smith, and students had their eyes rolling, as they remained calm during Akiko's and Jessica's exchanges.

After a short pause, Professor Smith proceeded to give a very short overview and historical background of Asia and the diversity among the 48 Asian countries. She saw that this was a great teaching and learning moment for her and her students.

She asked Akiko if she would not mind sharing a little bit about her Japanese culture. Akiko happily quipped, "China and Japan are not the same. Japanese culture is thousands of years old. The video game Pokémon is not the best representation of Japanese culture. We have great cuisine, many historical sites and theatrical shows, advanced technology, and many Japanese traditions."

Akiko's participation was both insightful to students and therapeutic to her. The clarification she provided made her feel proud to have redeemed her Japanese ancestors.

FRAMING THE PROBLEM

Akiko Matsumoto and Jessica Walberg are both students in a health and wellness course at a midwestern research university. Other than attending the same class, Akiko and Jessica never had a chance to meet and learn about one another.

Calling Akiko Chinese may be indicative of Jessica's lack of exposure and intercultural competence, which, at her young age, she still has time to develop given the right educational opportunities and exposure to others.

There are, nonetheless, many lessons to draw from this seemingly simple scenario that occurs quite often on and off college campuses.

It is true that host institutions and well-informed U.S. citizens celebrate the published statistics about the contributions of international students to the U.S. economy. American colleges and universities, however, still need to play a more proactive educational role in supporting and advocating for international students to decrease negative stereotypes and increase the intercultural competence of their graduates.

One way to increase awareness about the vital role international students at U.S. institutions play is through exposure to curricular and co-curricular programs that involve international students and scholars.

DISCUSSION QUESTIONS

1. What examples of curricular programs will help U.S. citizens become better informed about international students and international education?
2. What examples of co-curricular programs will help bring together international and domestic students, faculty, and staff?
3. Is raising awareness about the "the other" the responsibility of university diversity and equal opportunity officers alone?
4. What role do students play to help save face for an offended minority student in a class setting?
5. What role should professors play to correct wrong information about a minority group? [Many social scientists agree that there is a correlation between negative stereotypes and mistreatment of others. Professor Jaakko Lehtonen contends, "Negative cultural stereotypes and xenophobia may feed each other and give rise to a vicious circle: antagonism towards foreigners gives birth to negative stereotypical attributions, which, in turn, justify and boost negative feelings towards their cultural groups" (Lehtonen, 2013).]
6. What led Jessica to think that Akiko Matsumoto was culturally Chinese?
7. How can such cultural stereotype be avoided in any context, college campuses included?
8. What does Jessica's Pokémon comment reveal about American youth?
9. How could Akiko's reaction be interpreted?
10. Should taking courses in world history, world geography, and intercultural communication be required for graduation from U.S. colleges and universities?
11. In what ways could study-abroad opportunities help students become more culturally competent world citizens?

12. Is the U.S. government doing enough to help educate Americans about the rest of the world?
13. What can we learn from international students at American colleges and universities?

REFERENCES

Institute of International Education. (2017). www.iie.org

Jourdini, M. (2014). *The impact of international students on American students and faculty at an Appalachian university*. Germany: Scholars Press.

Lehtonen, J. (2013, October 18). Stereotypes and collective identification. Retrieved from https://moniviestin.jyu.fi/ohjelmat/hum/viesti/en/ics/16

Open Doors. (2017). www.iie.org

TWENTY

Did Implicit Bias Further Disenfranchise an Underrepresented Student?

Leah Robinson and De'Andrea Matthews

Rahel, a 28-year-old female medical student, attended the first *Population, Patient, and Physician* didactic of the year at a midwestern public medical school. This course teaches students cultural competence, medical ethics, evidence-based medicine, human sexuality, preventative medicine, public health interviewing, and physical diagnosis.

As one of eight students in the group, she looked around the room and noticed that she and one other student were the only non-White individuals in the group. While she did not know anyone in her group, at least two people knew each other from undergrad and three other students carpooled together.

While taking attendance, Dr. Marks studied the list of student names. The lecture topic for that day was documenting a patient's written history and physical examination, also known as an H&P. An H&P involves talking to the patient and gathering information about their current medical complaint, past medical history, lifestyle, and physical examination at the time of admission. The H&P also outlines the plan for addressing the issue that prompted the patient to visit the medical facility. It is then communicated to all providers involved in the care of that patient.

Communication skills are important and necessary to extract information from a patient as well as sharing it with the rest of the medical team. Taking a good H&P takes a considerable amount of practice. Knowing what to include and what to leave out depends on experience, but also an understanding of pathophysiology and illness. It requires a good technique that combines observational skills, listening skills, and integrating details from the patient's medical record.

88

The patient's medical record is rich with detail and information. Patients assume doctors are familiar with their individual content. The first time with a patient is essentially breaking the ice with a stranger. Rapport building is necessary to establishing the patient-physician relationship.

Dr. Marks explained that in a large urban setting in which the School of Medicine is situated, there are sizeable concentrations of health disparities that affect specific populations. In this particular case, Dr. Marks focused on the health disparities of African Americans. Attempting to pull a student's personal experience into the lesson on personal histories, the preceptor stated to the group while looking at Rahel, "You must be African *African* and not African *American.*" Taken slightly aback by the comment, Rahel froze and did not say anything for the remainder of the class.

Without confirmation from the student about her identity, Dr. Marks began to talk to the class about the difference between "African Africans" and African Americans, citing differences in diet and the history of slavery as discerning factors between the two groups. Throughout the duration of the didactic, Dr. Marks led the exchange with assumptions about the student's ethnicity and cultural identity while explaining various aspects of the patient history and physical. No other student's cultural background was brought into the conversation via questions or remarks.

Rahel felt uncomfortable being the reference point of the lecture. Upon further reflection, she thought that it was inappropriate. However, since it was the first day of class, she did not want to get off on the wrong foot with her preceptor or peers. She recognized that Dr. Marks had power and influence. Since he was also a residency director, he could write her a powerful letter of recommendation when the time came. Rahel had four years remaining to interact with Dr. Marks.

Rahel observed that no one else in the group said anything during Dr. Marks's lecture. She did notice that a few students looked uncomfortable, while others did not react at all. Rahel discussed the incident afterward with other classmates, some who had similar cultural backgrounds as she did. When she retold the story, her classmates were equally beleaguered by the comparison. Their reactions varied from mild irritation to being quite upset.

Rahel met with an academic advisor to talk about academic support as she was struggling in one class. She told the advisor that she did not know who to talk to and that a classmate recommended that she reach out to him, the African-American advisor in the Office of Diversity and Inclusion. The student explained that while she felt that the preceptor was not malicious, she felt isolated and uncomfortable. The student said, "Slavery existed in both Africa and America. I have never heard of African African." The student could not understand how or why the preceptor made such a distinction between the two groups or why she had been singled out.

The student also disclosed that she identifies as African American, having grown up in the Midwest. She said, "I have only been to Africa once, three years ago. And that is *beside* the point!" The student said, "I did not know what to do or what to say because the preceptor has power; he is in charge. On the first day, I did not want to give the wrong impression and upset him." If she did say something to the preceptor, she was concerned that she would come across as the "angry Black woman."

The advisor restated Rahel's account and asked for clarity to make sure he had heard her correctly. He wanted to know what type of support she needed to resolve this issue. Rahel stated, "I did not know how to handle the situation. I still don't." The advisor summarized key concepts of what was heard and listed them as follows: unequal power dynamic between student and professor, assumption of ethnic identity, bias, stereotyping, and stereotype threat. He then offered four ways to counter the situation while allowing the student to remain professional: ownership, humor, facts, and allyship.

OWNERSHIP

The advisor affirmed that Rahel had the right to claim her identity as she chooses. In owning her own identity through her language, she could have selected verbal self-defense to take ownership in any dialogue that took place. In the advisor's example, she could have said, "What I am willing to share with you is . . . " as a way of reclaiming her right to choose the culture with which she most closely identifies. How a student frames her experience and how she chooses to disclose personal and possibly sensitive information can create a powerful teachable moment toward a more culturally competent learning environment.

HUMOR

Another example was to frame the student's comments to say, "Based on my limited experience as . . . ," which provides a space to respect herself and an example for others to follow. In using humor, Rahel could have stated, "Dr. Marks, I have never heard of an African *African*. I am going to have to ask around about that one and run it through Google." The advisor smiled and said, "My father always says, humor is 50% of the truth." The advisor suggested, "When taken aback, reframe the narrative in a challenge of something new to learn. It encourages both parties to be open to the possibility of different ideas. This lessens the threat of retaliation as defenses are minimized through the use of humor."

FACTS

Another method is to overwhelm them with facts. The focus of medical education is an evidence-based solution to close the gap on health disparities. Unequal treatment, limited access, environmental factors, and social determinants are all avenues to be explored. The true prevalence of cognitive bias is unknown; however, pursuing how this bias can impact medical decisions should be presented as factual evidence. Asking to clarify statements and return to previous conversations for continuity, integration of new information learned, and completeness are aspects of academic discourse that should be embraced by any profession. Medicine, as a competency of lifelong learning, embraces research and data-driven outcomes. Provide the scholarship and reference around the facts in question.

ALLYSHIP

What about the role of stigma as it relates to patients, women, minorities, and the impoverished who face additional bias in hospital settings? Analyze the situation through multiple perspectives to make sure that the diagnosis or evaluation is comprehensive and inclusive enough. More than 50% of physicians come from wealth (Grumbach, 2011). Wealth has a way of clouding judgment in that it does not taken into account multiple perspectives along the social economic strata. In building a more comprehensive examination, ask for others' experience representative of the other economic tiers to add to the discussion.

A week later the counselor followed up with an email to Rahel that included an article on cognitive errors in diagnosis and strategies as an academic anchor. The article related cognitive bias with corrective measures. Physicians make errors due to cognitive biases. Being aware of cognitive bias and how to counteract it is crucial.

FRAMING THE PROBLEM

Dr. Marks, the preceptor for the session, is a physician with a long-established career at the university and in the community. Dr. Marks is White, over 60, comes from a family of physicians, and is married to a physician. His medical specialty is endocrinology with clinical research in diabetes. He has been teaching this course for at least 10 years.

Dr. Marks made an assumption about a student and exposed the class to bias, privilege, and paternalism. By not asking the student for confirmation of her ethnic identity, he used an unreliable method of assuming the student's ethnic identity simply by reading the student's name. In not asking Rahel for permission to use her as an example in the class discussion, he isolated and disengaged her from fully and actively participating. Dr. Marks took further liberties with generalizing his experiences as a legitimate viewpoint. Unfortunately, this modeled a behavior for other students, future physicians, and academicians to follow.

People of color (POC) are often underrepresented in the graduate classroom, particularly in the disciplines of science, technology, engineering, mathematics, and medicine (STEMM); however, these students should not carry the burden of representing the whole group. While the presence of underrepresented students is refreshing, it often provides teachable moments for Whites at the expense of being a live specimen. Powerlessness is stage 1 of six stages of personal power, as described by author Janet Hagberg (2002). Fear is the predominant factor at this stage that keeps the person in the stance as a victim. Finding allies and developing the necessary skills is the catalyst to move through the remaining stages of association, achievement, reflection, and purpose to ultimately embrace the power of wisdom.

DISCUSSION QUESTIONS

1. Does the counselor have any responsibility in reporting his consultation with Rahel? Why? What organizational structure exists at your institution to handle this type of situation?
2. Does "African African" exist as a cultural identity? What is the difference between ethnicity, race, and cultural identity? Who gets to claim it?
3. Rahel felt powerless. In what other ways could that feeling of powerlessness have been reframed?
4. Is silence detrimental to the collegiate experience? If so, how?
5. What is bystander apathy? What role could Rahel's classmates have played?

Editors' Note: This case is based on real student-professor interactions, but the names have been changed to protect the identities of those involved.

REFERENCES

Council of Graduate Schools. (N.d.). *Overview of research on underrepresented populations in graduate schools*. Retrieved from http://cgsnet.org/cgs-occasional -paper-series/memphis-university/part-1.

Croskerry, P. (2003). The importance of cognitive errors in diagnosis and strategies to minimize them. *Academic Medicine, 78*(8), 775–80.

DeAngelis, T. (2009). *Unmasking "racial micro aggressions."* Retrieved on December 1, 2017, from http://www.apa.org/monitor/2009/02/microaggression.aspx.

Grumbach, K. (2011). Commentary: Adopting postbaccalaureate pre-medical programs to enhance physician workforce diversity. *Academic Medicine, 86*(2), 154–157. doi:10.1097/ACM.0b013e3182045a68

Hagberg, J. O. (2002). *Real power: Stages of personal power in organizations.* Kenosha County, WI: Sheffield Publishing Company.

TWENTY-ONE

First-Generation Students Need Professors to Understand Them Better

Ginny Whitehouse

My student could barely lift his head as he said, "How can I focus on linear algebra if I don't know whether my Mom has eaten today?" In that moment, we both had an epiphany. He realized, without any prompting from me, that the best way out of destabilizing poverty was to stay in college. I realized that I had to teach differently . . . very differently.

First-generation college students bring with them the hopes and dreams of their entire communities, but without the tool kit of privileges other students bring. They arrive on college campuses without the support of parental knowledge to help navigate success. College GPA is not and should not be the only marker of academic achievement; nonetheless, it is one of the most prominent. First-generation students are more likely than their peers to need remedial courses, feel unprepared for college, and have a lower GPA (Pascarella, Pierson, Wolniak, & Terenzini, 2004).

The realities of university life may run counter to the students' prior experience:

- No, you can't get an excused absence to take your mother to the doctor.
- Sure, you are only in class 12 hours a week, but that doesn't mean you can also do a 40-plus-hour-a-week job and expect to pass.
- You cannot get a test postponed to bail your brother out of jail and get him admitted into rehab.
- In order to get a paid job after graduation, you need to work in an unpaid internship now.

- Your professor rolls his or her eyes when you say you didn't do an assignment described in the textbook because you have not bought the book. Then the eyes roll again when you have to work and cannot do an evening extra-credit opportunity in its place.
- Responding defiantly to a professor may feel justified, but it's the quickest way to get thrown out of class or even college.

First-generation college students may have been the best and brightest of their high schools. They may arrive with plans to major in three disparate fields so that they can keep their options open. They may have never had to study before to get good grades and have a rude awakening when they learn just how incredibly different college expectations may be. And their parents, who have been their role models, may not have the skill set to share the needed coping mechanisms.

Parents may give, frankly, bad advice. The astronomy lab is across campus and meets after dark. Parental advice: Just don't go. Work-study does not pay the bills? Parental advice: Take an off-campus job that offers more hours. Family crisis? Come home and skip Friday classes.

Meanwhile, parents may accuse their students of seeing themselves as somehow "better" than the rest of the family; parents simultaneously want their student to be successful and hold too tightly to maintain control (Storlie, Mostade, & Duenyas, 2016). These stressors create for the student something researchers call family achievement guilt, a significant angst not that different from survivors' guilt (Covarrubias & Fryberg, 2015).

The more differences students perceive in their identity and the identity of others in the classroom, the more knocks to their confidence. These lists of differences extend beyond first-generation and ethnicity; they include gender and orientation, immigration status, income level, learning style, and so on. Each knock makes it that much more challenging to speak up.

FRAMING THE PROBLEM

Professors coming from middle- to upper-class backgrounds often don't understand how their erroneous assumptions can crush student success. These statements are simply false and/or destructive:

- All students entering the university know how to read critically and identify key facts.
- Participation indicates preparation; therefore, students should be marked down for not speaking up in class discussions.

- Students needing assistance should be able to come to the professor's office during office hours and state clearly, quickly, and respectfully what aspect of material confuses them.
- Students should be able to do homework every night and know that they cannot cram before a test to do well.
- Students who fail simply do not have a good work ethic and are lazy.

These assumptions create roadblocks for first-generation students. Professors may define first-generation students more by what they don't do (ask for help) than by any other distinguishing characteristic (Horowitz, 2017). Entering higher education can be an uphill battle, but it is a battle that can be won.

Students can succeed, and I have been fortunate enough to observe many make it. That student who was worried about his mother is now Dr. Danjuma Quarless, a senior scientist doing human genetics research in the pharmaceutical industry. I asked him, "Tell me what professors get wrong about first-generation students."

Here's what he wrote:

Professors should know that a student's prior experience impacts their ability to complete their college education. Often, first-generation students fall toward the end of the performance distribution, not purely because of a lowered education aptitude or intellectual capacity, but more that the cumulative sum of "equities" is underdeveloped: financial equity, social equity, cultural equity, university-specific equity, etc. In many cases, these equities determine students' abilities to navigate their surroundings successfully.

First-generation students may be overwhelmed by these inequities long before any education or intellectual deficiencies take hold. Professors exacerbate these inequities when they treat all students as equally prepared, because it's the simplest model to teach and it requires no extra effort to individualize the curriculum to student needs. They need to employ some empathy in their agenda because of the inequities, and employ more than one modality to measure student learning. If the student can't complete that one modality, then the student fails or gets reduced marks.

The last mistake I'll bring up: Professors project their experience with learning and education on all students equally. Professors are professors because they were great at learning, and by that definition, may not empirically understand the individual who struggles in academics, such as the first-generation student.

A professor can make a difference in the lives of first-generation students by addressing inequities. Each student's level of preparation cannot be assumed, and spending time on the college tool kit helps everybody. Here are some possibilities:

- Include multiple types of assessment measures in classes, not just tests and oral responses in class.
- Teach how to memorize. Really.
- Offer a sample study schedule. Not just for lower-division, first-year classes, but for upper-division classes, too.
- Teach critical reading inside class time. Give time to read and break down a complex text. Students need to be taught how to chunk information into manageable parts.
- Encouraging students to tinker with an issue is a great way to teach problem solving unless that student walks into the classroom with low self-confidence. Give students the tools needed to understand options to solve problems.
- Pay attention to who leans in during small-group discussions and who pulls away. Consider why some students may disengage and evaluate alternatives to make everyone successful in the exercise.
- In review sessions, do not repeat information in the exact same way it was covered in class. If students didn't get it the first time, repeating won't help.
- Make yourself accessible if you can. Critically examine yourself and consider how you can make yourself more approachable.
- Move office hours, at least sometimes, to a neutral location, such as the campus coffee shop.
- Don't assume that a good student knows he or she is good. Encourage. Praise. Talk about graduate school. A small amount of encouragement goes a long way.

Here is the biggest thing: Professors should tell their own stories. Students often don't know what it takes to become a professor. They should talk about their own knocks. They may be perceived as having privileges that they do not believe they have. The only way to correct those misconceptions is to address them head on. Share the deficiencies. Let students know how hard professors had to work and how long it took to get their degrees.

First-generation students may experience a different kind of fear because they don't have role models to explain and shepherd their college years. They don't have a parent to say, "I had a bad first semester, too." Instead, they may be hearing, "You are just wasting our money." They have all kinds of doubts: Can I even get through college if I have never seen anybody else do it?

And going to talk with a professor about a bad grade may be the most frightening thing a first-generation student has have ever had to do. More than confronting a supervisor at work. More than bailing someone out of jail.

If you are having trouble getting students to come to your office hours, consider whether you might want to role-play in class what an office hour visit might look like. Showing the students what happens can reduce fear and help eliminate some of those confidence knocks.

You can make a difference in the lives of first-generation students, but to do so, you may have to change yourself. Here is the kicker: First-generation students make universities better because they are more likely than traditional students to challenge both the information-transfer model of teaching and possibly even the subject content itself (Chaffee, 1992). They are not burdened with the presumption that instruction must be top-down because it always has been. Their questions may come not from ignorance but from the fresh eyes of clarity.

DISCUSSION QUESTIONS

1. How is your educational experience similar to and different from the students in your classroom? How might those differences impact student learning?
2. Is giving structured assignments coddling students? Do "spelled out" instructions help students prepare for the real world? What might be an alternative view?
3. Think about your last three interactions with first-generation students. What did you hear that might be defining the distinctiveness of their experience? How could you have responded in a way that would be supportive rather than dismissive?
4. What kinds of incentives and rewards can/should be offered for talking with the professor? What physical and emotional barriers exist to making those meetings happen?
5. What can your institution do to better prepare the parents of first-generation students for the challenges their children face in college?
6. What can you do differently during class to make knowledge more accessible to everyone?

Editors' Note: *Dr. Danjuma Quarless gave permission for his story to be used.*

REFERENCES

Chaffee, J. (1992). Transforming educational dreams to educational reality. *New Directions for Community Colleges, 80*, 81–88.

Covarrubias, R., and Fryberg, S. A. (2015). Movin' on up (to college): First-generation college students' experiences with family achievement guilt. *Cultural Diversity & Ethnic Minority Psychology, 21*(3), 420–29.

Horowitz, G. (2017). First-generation college students: How to recognize them and be their ally and advocate. *Journal of College Science Teaching, 46*(6), 8–9.

Pascarella, E. T., Pierson, C. T., Wolniak, G. C., and Terenzini, P. T. (2004). First-generation college students: Additional evidence on college experiences and outcomes. *Journal of Higher Education, 75*(3), 249–84.

Storlie, C., Mostade, S. J., and Duenyas, D. (2016). Cultural trailblazers: Exploring the career development of Latina first-generation college students. *Career Development Quarterly, 64*(4), 304–17.

TWENTY-TWO

White Privilege

The Equity of Not Using the N-Word

Kirsten LaMantia and Holly Wagner

An all-White class was set to begin discussing privilege and oppression. The White professor, Dr. Jackson, prefaced this talk with exploring the cultural identities of each student and creating classroom activities to help foster a sense of safety and openness to vulnerability. Dr. Jackson also spent time on the first day of class asking students how they wanted to address intentional or unintentional problematic language used within the classroom. The students agreed that they wanted the professor to point out opportunities for growth in front of the class so that others could learn from it.

Dr. Jackson started the discussion by asking the students to begin to explore what their own Whiteness meant and if it impacted their experiences in the world. One student, Jane, said that though she could understand where there were some times she experienced privilege as a White woman, she also believed there were times life was unfair because she was White.

The professor asked for an example.

Jane said, "Well, I hear Black people say the N-word all the time. But then I'm not supposed to use it either? I think it's a power play against White people."

The professor asked the rest of the class what they thought about what Jane shared. Some of the other students nodded in agreement, and one said, "Yeah, it just seems like we should all have the same rules. That's equality." Dr. Jackson told the class she noticed some people weren't nodding and asked them to share their perspectives.

The other students explained that they had always been taught that they should not use the N-word, but they were not sure why. Dr. Jackson briefly lectured about the reclamation of words used to further marginalize and oppress vulnerable populations. Dr. Jackson explained that words that were once used to demean could be reclaimed by the marginalized group and used instead to empower and lift up.

Although the students seem to understand what she was saying, Dr. Jackson was just unsure if she was able to get through to them. Before the next class, Dr. Jackson asked her students to read the article titled "Straight Talk about the N-Word" by Sean Price (2011). This article explained the history of the N-word, the intricacies of it, and the consequences of using it.

Dr. Jackson was unsure if her class was able to differentiate between a person of color choosing a relationship with a derogatory term versus a White person's ability to have an opinion on that same word. She tried to speak with her class about how it was not up to the privileged or oppressor to determine how the marginalized or repressed related to a word. Dr. Jackson then remembered a speech the renowned author Ta-Nehisi Coates had recently given about this very topic. She searched for a video of it online and showed it to her class.

In this video (2017), Coates is asked by a White student how to explain to other White students that it was wrong to use the N-word. Coates explained that not every word is for everybody. He outlines his ability to differentiate between his wife referring to other women as bitches and him not being allowed to use that same word in the same way. He uses that commonality to appeal to his White audience to look at the language that they choose to use and the relationship their cultural identities have with that said word.

Dr. Jackson asked the students to think about the article they were given and what they heard from Ta-Nehisi Coates.

The next week Dr. Jackson asked her class what meaning they were making about their discussions about the use of the N-word. The students then shared how the word held more meaning than what they originally thought. Jane said, "I feel a little embarrassed about what I said in the other class. Now that I've heard from other people's perspectives, especially Black people's perspectives, I realize why I can't use the N-word."

Some of the other people in the class shared how their opinions on the use of the N-word had changed as well.

FRAMING THE PROBLEM

Dr. Jackson is a nontenured professor at a small university in a rural, conservative area. She is discussing the reality of White privilege with her all-White class. Some of the students are having trouble identifying how they have experienced privilege personally, especially the White student who grew up in severe poverty. A few weeks into the class, the topic was the language that the oppressed and the oppressors have used. Several students expressed their confusion about the ability to use the N-word. This spurred a deeper conversation regarding social norms surrounding reclaimed versus offensive language.

DISCUSSION QUESTIONS

1. How do you think Dr. Jackson handled Jane's comment about not being able to use the N-word?
2. Do you agree with Jane's idea that "we should all have the same rules" for there to be equality?
3. What do you think about the reclamation of the N-word by some people of color, and how would you articulate your perspective to your students?
4. Do you draw comparisons from this with other words that have been reclaimed by oppressed populations (ex. *Queer* within LGBTQQIA populations)? Why or why not?
5. What other resources would you have used to facilitate classroom discussion on systemic oppression, racism, and inequality regarding reclamation and linguistics?

Editors' Note: *This case study represents the real experiences of a professor, but some of the details are a composite, and some have been changed slightly to protect the identity of the students.*

REFERENCES

Coates, T. (2017). *We were eight years in power book tour.* Lecture, Family Action Network Event with Evanston Township High School.
Price, S. (2011). Straight talk about the N-word. *Teaching Tolerance, 40.*

TWENTY-THREE

Diversity Issues for Faculty

"What Do You Think?" Inclusion/ Exclusion Dynamics in Group Work

Eleni Oikonomidoy

The integration of collaborative group work is one of the multiple methods that faculty who aim to have creative, inclusive, and student-centered college classrooms implement. However, the nuances of group work are not always straightforward—particularly when students come from different cultural backgrounds.

Being aware of this reality, Professor X always tries hard to create an environment of acceptance and civic responsibility in the classroom. Given that the class deals with challenging issues of diversity and equity in schools, her aim is to model a classroom environment that validates diverse students' ways of being and promotes equity. She goes to great lengths to do so.

The first day of classes and prior to the review of the syllabus, she invites the students to create together the guidelines that will be used to guide classroom instruction. She first divides the class in small groups and then asks students to share their recommendations and vote which ones they would like to implement in the large group. She mediates the oftentimes vague suggestions by highlighting the importance of culture in their interpretations.

For instance, the students many times propose that a guiding force of the classroom interactions should be respect. Professor X asks the students to define what they mean by respect and to contemplate whether its expressions are the same across different cultural contexts.

After the discussion, the students are asked to identify what the meaning of respect will be in the context of the classroom interactions—both face-to-face and online. Periodically throughout the semester, Professor X invites the students to review the guidelines that they created on the first day and make necessary adjustments. They know that the document is always in progress as the group navigates through multiple interactions.

In addition, Professor X tries to model the acceptance that she espouses when responding to students' comments and questions. She acknowledges all responses and gently invites the students to reconsider or interrogate assumptions that may underlie their statements, both written and oral.

In so doing, she encourages the students to use a similar gentle tone in their interactions with one another and to implement a critical lens in analyzing various social and educational phenomena. For the most part, the students appear to appreciate this process and emulate similar behaviors and attitudes.

The above characteristics guided instruction during the spring academic semester. Professor X was happy with the progress that the students were making and was pleased to observe critical engagement and constructive tensions during group work (Parker, 2004). On this particular day, the groups had been assigned to discuss the chapters that were due using the guiding questions that she provided for them. She walked around the room, consulting with various groups about the topics that they were bringing up and answering clarifying questions about the material examined.

As she was on the one side of the room talking to the small group, she continued to look around to ensure that no hands were raised eliciting her presence and assistance. Her glaze stopped at the group that was located on the other side of the room. A tension seemed to have escalated there if she was to judge from the body language and the intensity/loudness of one of the members' voice. She wrapped up her point quickly and moved to that side of the room.

Kayla, who was an African-American female, continued to talk in a rather loud voice. She seemed to address only one of the members of her five-member group: a European-American female, Natasha.

She told her, "I don't need anyone telling me when I should talk and when not. I am here for my own learning and I don't need you to tell me what to do."

The other student responded, "I just wanted to make sure that you take part in the group work. I didn't want to ignore your valuable insights. I just asked what your thoughts are."

Professor X moved closer to the group and inquired about the situation.

Kayla explained that she was being forced to contribute to the small-group discussion when she had no intention of talking. Natasha added that she just wanted to include her peer and not make her feel excluded.

Soon after that, tears started to emerge in her eyes. She left the room. Everyone else in the group did not say a word. Professor X was flabbergasted. At first she thought to comfort Natasha, who was still crying upon her return to the class. However, she immediately sensed that such an action could be perceived as "taking sides," so she withdrew. Luckily, the assigned group work time was concluding, and it was time for a transition to the break.

Professor X took the opportunity to invite the two students to take a deep breath and to talk to her individually when they were ready. She made it clear that she wanted to hear from both sides, in the absence of other students' staring eyes. The second part of the instruction passed. Natasha came to Professor X to explain her intentions right after class. Professor X went to Kayla to inform her that she would like to talk to her as well.

Natasha explained that she was quite conscious of circumstances in which members of underrepresented groups are "silenced" in classroom interactions. She admitted that her delivery may have been too direct, but her intention was to validate her classmate's expected contributions to the discussion and not leave her out of the group.

Professor X indicated her understanding and discussed the nuances associated with cross-cultural interactions. She also invited her to check in with her prior to the following class.

Kayla appeared to be still quite bothered by the interaction when she talked to Professor X. She stated, "I don't need nobody telling me when to talk." Professor X validated her reaction and, like Natasha, indicated the nuances associated with cross-cultural interactions, in this case being keenly aware of the power differentials between the two students.

The following week without instruction seemed to have a healing effect on the interaction. Both students seemed to have reflected on the event when they came back to the classroom. After checking with the professor individually, they addressed each other courteously and gave their hands. Natasha promised to never put Kayla in the uncomfortable position to talk when she did not want to, and Kayla apologized for her tone.

FRAMING THE PROBLEM

Kayla was an active participant to the classroom discussions prior to that Monday. She was engaged both with the material and with her peers. That one day, she did not want to participate. Natasha, who was similarly engaged, took it upon herself to invite her classmate to talk.

Was the incident a case of a cross-cultural misunderstanding, a potentially unconscious patronizing, or a microaggression?

DISCUSSION QUESTIONS

1. How often do you think scenarios like the one above take place in classrooms, meetings, and other spaces in campuses?
2. In your view, how could the professor respond alternatively to the situation at hand? Were there any specific actions that you found effective/ineffective? Which ones and why?
3. Assumptions about group work and collaborative learning spaces oftentimes seem to ignore cultural communication styles that value silence and observation. What is the meaning of these?
4. What could be some underlying reasons why Kayla did not want to participate in classroom discussion that particular day? Could it be that she was having a bad day? Had a headache? Did not have time to complete the readings? Did not find the readings engaging? Could a different cultural framework assist in interpreting each one? Which ones?
5. What types of training should faculty in all academic disciplines receive in order to be somewhat prepared for the unexpected consequences of group work?

Editors' Note: *This case study is based on a real-world situation, but the names and some details have been changed to protect the identities of the students.*

REFERENCE

Parker, W. C. (2004). Diversity, globalization, and democratic education: Curriculum possibilities. In J. Banks (Ed.), *Diversity and citizenship education: Global perspectives* (433–58). San Francisco: Jossey-Bass.

UNIT 3
POLICY ISSUES

TWENTY-FOUR

Students Are Anxious, Divided over Bathroom Policies

Sherwood Thompson

A tall and skinny, bald-headed African-American professor named Dr. Harris was addressing a question posed by a Hispanic student in class. The student had asked whether transgender students should be allowed to use the restrooms of their choice on campus. He wondered if the university was discriminating against transgender students by denying this choice.

Professor Harris pondered for a moment before telling the class a personal story. He recounted his own childhood, during which African Americans had to use the "Negro only" bathrooms. He confided in them that those facilities were often filthy and smelly; they were undesirable because they were rarely cleaned. Although he and his family would have preferred to use cleaner bathrooms, they were restricted due to Jim Crow segregation laws and states' rights. Professor Harris then asked the class to discuss the Hispanic student's questions regarding transgender rights.

Erin, an exchange student, passionately argued that it is silly to prohibit any individual from any bathroom. She asked her fellow students to consider what she determined to be the triviality of this debate and even challenged Americans to "grow up."

Faye, an African-American student, agonized with Professor Harris over the painful history of segregation in America. She told the class that her parents and grandparents in the Jim Crow South would literally run down busy business streets in their town if they had to go in public, rushing toward the city courthouse to use the bathroom. They made the quick dash because the courthouse held the only bathroom that African Americans could legally use. Her mother had told her that then, if an African-American person, young or old, was forced to discharge waste on the sidewalk or a grassy area of the street, he or she could be arrested and fined for indecent exposure. She concluded, "Why not use a bathroom, any bathroom, if you got to go?"

Randy, a White student, was disgusted by the idea of a transgender person standing next to him at the urinal. He said he would campaign against the rights of "others" using the wrong bathroom. "Let them use the bathroom that relates to the sex on their birth certificate. That's the proper gender of a person."

Jimmy, a transgender student, was obviously upset by the comments made in class. Jimmy spoke with urgency and said, "What about equal treatment and fairness? These are people we're talking about—real human beings. They are not dogs running around the yard looking for a convenient tree. The question here is a civil rights issue. Are some people going to exert their personal and political power over individuals who have a different sexuality? What about social justice and the right to be treated with simple dignity?" Jimmy reminded the class that transgender people have to stand up for equality: "This is America, isn't it? Who gave intolerant people the right to determine for me what I should want or be?"

After allowing these expressions, Professor Harris lectured, in classical style, on the origins of the bathroom policy. He referenced a *Time* magazine web article titled "Everything You Need to Know about the Debate over Transgender People and Bathrooms" by Katy Steinmetz (2015), which reveals that the bathroom policy has roots in the social conservative political movement in states such as Arizona, Maryland, North Carolina, Kentucky, and Florida. These policies typically mandate that people use the bathroom that coincides with the sex assigned on their birth certificates. He said the bathroom policy issue is popular within the same movement that denounces issues of sex education in public schools, that seeks to stop immigration in America, and that fights to repeal former President Obama's Affordable Health Care Act, commonly called Obamacare.

Professor Harris explained that proponents within the conservative movement believe that a bill restricting transgender bathroom rights and requiring proof of gender is necessary to protect the people's privacy and public safety (Williams, 2016, p. 1). Professor Harris balanced his talk by expressing that opponents of the bathroom bill are generally seeking "equal rights under the law."

Finally, Professor Harris informed the class regarding a recent ruling by the Fourth Circuit Court of Appeals of Virginia that required public schools to allow transgender students to use the bathroom that coincides with their gender identity rather than gender assignment, the first decision of its kind. As reported by Pete Williams with *U.S. News*, the decision is binding on the five states of the Fourth Circuit—Maryland, North and South Carolina, Virginia, and West Virginia (2016, p. 1).

The professor kept his lecture short and told the class that it is the responsibility of each individual to find accurate information and make an informed decision regarding this issue.

FRAMING THE PROBLEM

While lecturing in class, Professor Harris acknowledged a student who asked a question about the heavily debated "bathroom policy." Although responsive, the professor allowed a back-and-forth discussion among students in the class.

Several students gave their opinions about the "bathroom policy." They mentioned issues of sovereign rights, freedom, and privacy, and they shared their biases. The conversation was heated at times; nevertheless, Professor Harris interjected and shared research and court rulings that offered some qualitative information. He recommended to the students that they learn as much as they can about the issue and come to an intelligent decision for themselves.

DISCUSSION QUESTIONS

1. Do you think it was appropriate for Professor Harris to discuss the pros and cons of the bathroom bill question posed by one of his students?
2. How do you feel about the comments made by others students in the class? Do you think their comments were helpful in understanding this complex policy issue or just a bunch of mumbo jumbo?
3. Was Jimmy right in asking, "Who gave intolerant people the right to determine for me what I should want or be?" Do you think this question is a personal prerogative, a matter for the courts to decide, or a matter of personal social justice?
4. Do you believe that the ruling of the Fourth Circuit Court of Appeals of Virginia made the right decision? How do you think this decision will change the attitudes of people about transgender individuals and the bathroom usage issue?
5. Do you think that colleges and universities are the hybrid between what goes on in the wider society and on campus? Should a college or university work toward being a single community environment of learners or a collective community of many diverse worldviews with separate perspectives? Should colleges and universities be the guardians of equity and sexual security on campus?

Editors' Note: *This hypothetical scenario does not depict actual students or instructors, but rather, it represents the type of interactions that can occur on campuses across the country.*

REFERENCES

Steinmetz, K. (2015). Everything you need to know about the debate over transgender people and bathrooms. Retrieved from http://time.com/3974186/transgender-bathroom-debate/

Williams, P. (2016). Appeals court rules on transgender bathrooms in schools case. Retrieved from http://www.nbcnews.com/news/us-news/appeals-court-rules-transgender-bathroomrules-n558496

TWENTY-FIVE

Selective Flying

Is a Flag Truly Removed When It Still Shows Up on Game Day?

Willie R. Tubbs

As Mississippi fall Saturdays go, the one on which the Southern Miss Golden Eagles hosted the UTEP Miners for Homecoming 2017 was quite pleasant. With temperatures hovering around 82 degrees and the Gulf South humidity mercifully south of 70%, the announced crowd of 21,970 people watched the Golden Eagles secure a win.

It was, in virtually every way, a typical fall Saturday in the South, where for about four months each year, tens of thousands of fans routinely cram into college football stadiums to cheer on their teams and, in no small measure, reenact game day rituals that date back in some cases to the late 19th century.

The University of Southern Mississippi, founded in 1910 as Mississippi Normal College, is not the most aged Southern institution of higher education, but the school does not lack for traditions. On the Saturday in question, the sights and sounds of Golden Eagle football, which played its first game in 1912, might have been modernized by technology, but it had the air of times gone by (Southern Miss Football Media Relations, 2015).

The Pride of Mississippi Marching Band performed its set-in-stone and popular pregame show. "Top Fanfare" echoed to the top of the stadium, the Dixie Darlings dance team stomped and kicked its way onto the field to the tune of "Are You from Dixie?" Then, to the strains of "Battle Hymn of the Republic," a quartet of ROTC students presented the colors of the United States and the state of Mississippi.

As I rose, as is my custom, in honor of those whom serve, I was struck by the optics. While the United States flag has garnered much attention at stadiums the nation over—with sportscasters, news anchors, fans, and activists of all stripe enumerating and debating those who stand or kneel for the National Anthem—I couldn't help but think about the lesser-known flag, that of the state of Mississippi.

I was compelled to ask, "Why is this here?" The reason for my conundrum was that I had been led to believe, as had virtually everyone else, that the Mississippi state flag had been removed from the campus of USM in 2015. In fact, as of November 2016, no state college or university was flying the colors of Mississippi (Jaschik, 2016).

The flag of the Magnolia State is no stranger to controversy. As modern state flags go, it is objectively the most controversial. Mississippi is the last state flag to feature a representation of the Confederate flag in its overall design (Firestone, 2001). The Stars and Bars dominates the flag's appearance, set in the top left corner of the flag.

As I stood, hand to heart and silent, my mind was not on those who serve. As is my wont, and that of so many who work in academia, my mind switched to analysis mode. I pondered how the flag could be both removed and not removed at the same time. My mind didn't have too much time to dwell. The anthem ended, the colors were retired, and the game went on without another appearance of the state flag.

Days later, as I chatted with friends from the school, I asked them if they'd noticed that the flag was still popping up on game day. All admitted they'd seen it but not appreciated the significance of the reappearance. A quick pass over YouTube confirmed that the flag had appeared at other games since the 2015 removal. When I attended USM's spring commencement in 2017, the state flag made another appearance, again as part of a color guard.

On October 28, 2015, amid a growing cry for change from among many faculty and students, USM resident Dr. Rodney Bennett ordered the flag removed. "I am looking forward to a time when this debate is resolved and USM raises a state flag that unites us," Bennett said in a news release sent to state and local media (http://news.usm.edu/article/message-university-president-rodney-d-bennett-removal-state-flag).

This move was quite popular on campus and in the media but was by no means universally celebrated. In the years that have followed, Southern Miss has become home to weekly dueling protests over the flag. Every Sunday, a small group of pro- and antiflag activists report to their designated protest areas to mostly wave signs at passersby and speak ill of one another. And while select members of the two sides are fond of cursing at each other, there have been no outbreaks of violence. It is hard to stress how small both groups are. It would be hard for the two groups to stage a game of flag football.

These threats are largely toothless, to say nothing of impractical. It seems unlikely politicians would defund the entirety of state higher education over the display of a flag whose existence has split the state. That's a recipe for alienating virtually everyone in the state, to say nothing of being voted out of office. The temptation, then, is for the analyst to make a snap judgment and recommend the school remove the flag from every facet of its existence. While this is certainly an option, there are confounding factors that bear consideration.

Among the school's primary publics is the military. A long-standing tradition on game days is for the ROTC color guard to present the colors. While it would be simple to say "just don't have color guard anymore" or to require the ROTC to furl the state flag, to do so could expose the university to the same type of risks state legislators would face were they to make good on their threats.

The Southern Miss ROTC programs, army and air force respectively, have a rich history at the school, and both are well liked on and off campus. To cease having ROTC color guard, even if the ROTC program came out in support, would alienate a huge population on campus and, most likely, be branded antimilitary/antipatriotic in the community.

An unpopular fact, but a fact nonetheless, is that despite strong opposition to the Mississippi state flag, few citizens bother to protest or counterprotest in earnest. Anecdotally, and perhaps this is just a byproduct of the football-crazed nature of the South, I've heard of no one complaining about, much less organizing against, the flag at large events.

There have been instances in which students faced harsh criticism, and in at least one instance abuse, from classmates when they chose not to stand for the National Anthem at home football games, but no stories have arisen about pro- or antistate flag sentiment on game day. Perhaps people of all ilk are more interested, if only for three hours, in the game. Perhaps the brief nature of the flag's appearance makes it easy to forget.

FRAMING THE PROBLEM

How do you define *removed*? That seems a silly question. I hazard that virtually no one on a college campus would struggle to define the term. However, at the University of Southern Mississippi, the word seems to have lost some of its power. Two years ago, the school officially removed the state flag of Mississippi, as controversial a piece of cloth as you will find in the United States thanks to its being adorned with the flag of the Confederacy.

This move was largely popular, and the university was praised for removing a divisive symbol from its campus, but the flag makes appearances when the most eyeballs are present. The Mississippi flag might have been replaced by additional American flags at the front of campus, but it still makes appearances at large-scale events on campus.

When USM hosts a football game, the flag will be there. When the school celebrates a graduation, the flag will be there. The question begs, though, should it be? And should the school have been celebrated for its original decision? Should the university, and the others in Mississippi, have even removed the state flag at all? Have university administrators overstepped their bounds?

Lest anyone excoriate the institutions of higher education in Mississippi prematurely, the schools are in a no-win situation. Public sentiment on both the micro and macro level is split. While there is a growing "change the flag" movement in Mississippi, there are still plenty of Mississippians who want the flag to stay as is.

The most recent referendum on the state flag went in favor of staying the course. In 2001, the state held a referendum of sorts on the flag. I say of sorts, because the referendum did not ask, "Should Mississippi change its state flag?" but rather prompted voters to choose between the existing flag and a single new design.

Even on the Southern Miss campus, where the majority of faculty and staff prefer the flag's removal, there are still those who push for continuity. The leaders of the University of Southern Mississippi, facing pushes and pulls from every direction, made its play in 2015, and we are left to determine how much celebration was warranted and, ultimately, recommend what should be done in the future.

Why did Southern Miss act at all, and why did the school act in the way it did?

There are several possible solutions. Option 1, the pessimistic view, is that Southern Miss showed hollow courage by publicly "removing" the flag but still allowing for its display on game days and at graduations. One might even argue the school made a shallow grab at positive public relations and removed the flag in theory but allows for its display when the most people, and by extension the most power brokers, are on campus.

Option 2, the optimistic view, is that the university has taken a significant step forward, despite a split public and has thus behaved courageously. The optimist need not agree with the school's decision to appreciate that the change was done in an attempt to foster harmony.

There are many negotiated ways to read this situation. Perhaps the university's response is an attempt at negotiating a complicated sociopolitical landscape. The removal of the flag from the front of campus was a ceremonial act intended to please the antiflag group while the continued appearance of the flag at big events is an attempt to not further alienate those in favor of the flag.

DISCUSSION QUESTIONS

1. How do you read the university's response? Which, if any, of the two aforementioned options do you feel best describes the university's actions? Is there a third way to describe the situation?
2. How should the University of Southern Mississippi proceed on game days and at graduations? Would it be better to forego military color guards in favor of not displaying the flag or to maintain ties to the military by allowing ROTC to continue to display both the United States and the Mississippi state flag?
3. Has the university succeeded in uniting the community around the American flag, or has the decision to remove the Mississippi state flag further exacerbated the division?
4. Is the university's decision to allow pro- and anti-state flag groups equal space on Sundays sufficient in allowing for open discourse on the campus? Should the groups be allowed to demonstrate on additional days?
5. Does the state of Mississippi have the right to deny funding to universities that refuse to fly the state flag? If so, should the state apply such penalties?

REFERENCES

Firestone, D. (2001, April 18). Mississippi votes by wide margin to keep state flag that includes confederate emblem. *New York Times*. http://www.nytimes.com/2001/04/18/us/mississippi-votes-wide-margin-keep-state-flag-that-includes-confederate-emblem.html

Jaschik, S. (2016, November 4). Delta state takes down Mississippi flag. *Inside Higher Education*. Retrieved from https://www.insidehighered.com/quicktakes/2016/11/04/delta-state-takes-down-mississippi-flag

Leib, J. I., & Webster, G. R. (2012). Black, white or green? The Confederate battle emblem and the 2001 Mississippi state flag referendum. *Southeastern Geographer*, 52(3), 299–326.

Southern Miss Football Media Relations (2015). 2015 Southern Miss Quick Facts. Retreived from http://southernmiss.com/documents/2018/7/11/fb_quick_facts.pdf

USM News Release. (2015, October 28). http://news.usm.edu/article/message-university-president-rodney-d-bennett-removal-state-flag

TWENTY-SIX

Recognizing Institutional Betrayal on College Campuses

Doris W. Carroll

Professor Joseph Rockwell is, by all measures, a superstar in physics. He has more than 100 publications, five textbooks, and is in the middle of his second $5 million, multiyear NSF grant in five years. He has a fully equipped lab that supports five doctoral students, three males and two females, including Sara, a third-year physics doctoral student.

At the start of the year, Professor Rockwell met with all five doctoral students to discuss how to manage the new laboratory equipment and made assignments to support undergraduate physics students' research in the lab, a course requirement in the advanced physics class, which they each take turns coteaching over the course of two semesters.

Sara is uncomfortable being alone in Professor Rockwell's office because he has made sexual advances toward her, asking her to go out after class for a drink to "get acquainted better." Professor Rockwell is Sara's major advisor for her doctoral work. Her doctoral thesis research is contingent upon using the professor's lab.

Twice, Sara has refused his offer to go out for drinks with Professor Rockwell. Each time, Sara told him that she had grading to do. Sara is reluctant to tell him that she is uncomfortable with his request out of fear that she will lose her doctoral graduate research assistantship.

Last week, Professor Rockwell asked her to go out, and again Sara said no. This time Professor Rockwell remarked, "Well, you know that you need me to finish your doctoral thesis research in my lab. You should be nice to me. And then I'll help you finish your degree. If you don't say yes, I'll remove you from the lab. Then what!?"

Sara is scared and frustrated. So she confides to Arts and Sciences Assistant Dean Nate Williams whose responsibility includes research activities across the entire college. Assistant Dean Williams is sympathetic to her frustrations and suggests she go visit the campus Title IX coordinator to learn how best to manage this sexual harassment.

Then he remarks, "We cannot afford to lose Professor Rockwell's research monies right now. You have to find a way to deal with this situation."

FRAMING THE PROBLEM

Professor Rockwell has responsibilities to treat all his doctoral students fairly and equitably, in accordance with university policies and federal laws. Professor Rockwell is abusing his power as full professor and major advisor for his own personal gain. For Sara, his sexual advances create a hostile workplace, and that reality has compromised her safety and interfered with her GTA duties, and it now constrains her doctoral thesis research.

While Assistant Dean Williams did encourage Sara to consult with the Title IX coordinator about how to manage sexual harassment, he too should have called the Title IX coordinator to clarify his obligations to report this harassing incident. Assistant Dean Williams failed to do that.

Worse, his comment to Sara about not wanting to lose Professor Rockwell's research monies was an insult to her. Assistant Dean Williams's comments disregarded her fears and concerns about sexual harassment and her assigned roles as GTA and doctoral student. Assistant Dean Williams let Sara down, too. His comments invalidated her as a person. As members of the institutional community, both Professor Rockwell and Assistant Dean Williams contributed to a campus climate that permitted harassment to continue on this campus and go unchecked.

DISCUSSION QUESTIONS

1. How might Assistant Dean Williams have responded differently to Sara, in an equitable and fair manner, with actions that would support Sara and her allegations of sexual harassment?
2. What is Assistant Dean Williams's obligation to support the institution and their policies about sexual harassment? Did he fulfill his institutional obligation of care with Sara?
3. What should Dean Williams have done on behalf of Sara?
4. What should the institution do about Professor Rockwell's sexual advances to Sara? Which administrator should approach Professor

Rockwell about these allegations of problematic behavior that violates institutional policies?

5. What is the institution's responsibility to Sara to protect her safety?
6. What should Sara's academic department do to best support her to work, learn, and study in a safe manner?
7. How did Professor Rockwell fail in his supervisory obligations to Sara? What is the remedy for those failures?

Editors' Note: This case is one that the author created, and it represents an aggregate of experiences coming from her years in higher education.

REFERENCE

Smith, C. P., & Freyd, J. J. (2014). Institutional betrayal. *American Psychologist,* *69*(6), 575–87. http://dx.doi.org/10.1037/a0037564

TWENTY-SEVEN

Retention of Underrepresented Students

When Does Perseverance Hinder One's Ability to Compete?

Leah Robinson and De'Andrea Matthews

A large, midwestern, urban university requires that all students meet with an advisor during their first semester in college. Jared, a first-year college student, decides to get this requirement out of the way and goes to the advising center after the second week of classes. He reports to the advisor that everything is fine but finds himself incredibly tired after anatomy lab. During his conversation with the academic advisor, Mr. Douglas, the student reveals that he has a "thing with his hand and arm" that could be corrected with surgery. Mr. Douglas asks for more information about Jared's hand. The advisor warns Jared that his problem may become exacerbated as the anatomy lab progresses due to lab requirements of performing dissections, incisions, and cutting.

Jared reported seeing a nurse practitioner (NP) after the first week of classes. Writing notes and learning how to use the dissection tools, his hand was swollen and his wrist weak. He told the NP that he fell and caught himself on his hands several months ago. Not wanting to worry his mother, he did not mention how much pain he was in when it first happened. The nurse practitioner tells Jared to follow up with his doctor. The type of injury he had could need surgery that would require some weeks to recuperate. Without X-rays and a proper examination, the nurse could not tell Jared what was wrong with his hand. She did, however, write a refillable prescription for anti-inflammatories and advised him to ice his hand regularly, reminding him again to see a doctor.

The advisor asked about Jared's other classes, as he was carrying 16 credits in his first semester. Jared shrugged and said, "I've been focusing all my energy on anatomy because I never had that class before. I've had English and math and can pull it together for those courses. Math has never been a problem for me. English was OK, but I don't like to read that much."

Jared reported that there were no assignments due in either class. The first exam in math was at the end of the month. A draft of the first paper was due in English in two weeks. Jared could only afford the first two of the six books required for English. He and his roommate are in the same math course but different sections. His roommate lets him borrow the math text when he needs it.

The advisor tells Jared that the academic support center offers workshops on time management, college writing, and reading strategies. He also gives Jared a flier from financial aid on emergency loans and schedules another appointment around midterms. Jared thanks the advisor for his time and walks to his next class. Jared never makes an appointment with academic support.

Jared calls his mom every week to update her on his progress at school. He tells her what the advisor said about his hand and arm. The family has had sporadic health insurance coverage for the last several years. The last time Jared saw a doctor was for his physical during his sophomore year in high school. She attributed Jared's complaint about his arm and hand to growing pains as he shot up eight inches in the last six months. Jared's mom tells him to just push through; it's just anatomy. He persists but finds that anatomy is much more labor intensive than he expected. He finds that not only does he have to spend more time on anatomy, but in doing so, he continues to neglect his other courses.

Jared finds that drawing anatomical structures is very helpful to his learning process, but it is also very time consuming and intensifies due to his medical condition. Now in constant pain, he is getting little sleep trying to keep up. On the day of the exam, Jared finds out that there are two parts to complete: a written exam that is multiple choice and a practical exam that is short answer, requiring him to identify anatomical structures by name. The practical is a timed test that requires students to move to a new station every minute and identify the structure located at that station. The practical part of the exam counts twice as much as the written part. While he is pretty good at taking multiple-choice tests, he has little skill with short answer. During the practical portion, he gets frustrated because he did not see any structures that matched the lab manual.

Jared gets a 60% on the anatomy exams. He calculates that he needs a 74% on the next three exams to pass anatomy with a C, or 70%. Determined, Jared buckles down to conquer the next unit of materials. He gets a bad head cold the first week and a half of the new unit and is unable to participate in labs and lectures, so he falls behind in the unit. Afraid of disappointing everyone, Jared does not tell his family the outcome of the first set of exams, nor does he share with his roommate, friends, girlfriend, or lab group. Instead, he decides to video stream all the lectures and goes into the lab after hours alone.

On the second set of exams, Jared earns the same score of 60%. Keeping in mind that he was sick for part of the unit, he is perplexed that his score did not change at all despite being able to control his time due to video streaming. Jared now needs to get 80% on the next two exams in anatomy in order to pass with a 70%. Feeling slightly stronger and being very busy, he lets the prescription for his medications run out. He found an app that allows him to visualize all necessary anatomical structures for the next unit, which gives him confidence with the new material and reduces his need to draw everything out. Jared proceeds to attack the third unit in the same manner as he did the previous unit; however, on the third set of exams, he gets the same anatomy score of 60%. He crammed for math over the weekend and pulled off a B- on the first exam. The draft of his English paper was satisfactory, but it will need major revisions.

In order to pass the anatomy course with a 70%, he now needs to get 100% on the last exam. His medical condition flares up during the last week of unit three, but he still has not been able to renew his medications due to his busy schedule and limited funds. His girlfriend, Sheila, is coming to town for a visit they planned at the beginning of the academic year. She knows he has been having some difficulty in classes but assumes that, just like in high school, he has been able to pull things up.

When Sheila arrives on campus, Jared is in a bad mood, bloated from gaining 25 pounds, and his face is riddled with acne. She starts to talk about her studies, new friends, and scores from midterms with enthusiasm, expecting him to do the same. Jared barely responds to Sheila, getting angrier and more shut down as the visit progresses. By the end of the visit, the two are barely speaking to each other.

FRAMING THE PROBLEM

Jared is a first-generation college student from out of state. Away from home for the first time, he relies on his mother's advice, whom he respects, although she has never attended college. He must maintain full-time enrollment to maximize his financial aid and scholarship eligibility. He heard that people take a long time to finish because they only do the minimum credit load per semester. As such, he is carrying a 16-credit-hour load trying to make everyone proud by completing his undergraduate degree in the prescribed four years. The minimum full-time credit load at his university is 12 credits.

Jared is ashamed that he failed the first set of exams. That shame has caused him to isolate himself and not seek help. Formally, Jared could get help from the academic support center tutors, supplemental instruction leaders, or faculty members. Informally, Jared could study with a learning community, lab partners, or friends. He has never had to use tutoring in high school, as he often helped his friends at lunch time with math. Without much effort, Jared maintained a B+ average in high school and was considered smart by teachers and peers. Fearful of failing, Jared keeps his problems a secret, afraid that his peers will rebuff him and consider him a fraud.

According to the National Student Clearinghouse Research Center, the average length of time to complete an undergraduate degree is five to six years. The transition from high school to college is difficult for many students, particularly those who are the first in their family to go to college. Taking a lighter credit load the first semester is advantageous for many reasons, as there are several things to navigate and learn as a young adult. It is better to have great success with a few classes than struggle with a larger credit load.

Jared was focused on the course that was giving him the greatest challenge and neglecting the other courses. He needed to learn how to manage his time, balance course work with study, and use academic resources. Jared modeled the same academic behavior used in the past; however, it did not yield similar results. He assumed that his academic strengths from high school would be the same in college. They were not, and he did not adjust appropriately or in a timely manner.

Along with basic survival skills, asking for and receiving academic help is not easy for individuals who are used to helping others. More importantly, since Jared has limited experience asking for help, for him, needing help is often considered a sign of weakness. While 70% is considered passing, earning above 85% is considered advantageous toward mastery of the course material. Introductory courses build the foundation for future courses. Jared would not be able to move on to the next level of anatomy without repeating the course. Repeating courses is costly and affects scholarship and financial aid eligibility. If he is a science or premed major, his poor performance may place him on academic probation after the first semester. Such an outcome could cause him to drop out.

Jared needs to be around a group of peers who can model correct behaviors and introduce him to resources and key personnel necessary for his success.

DISCUSSION QUESTIONS

1. What is perseverance and how does it teach students to handle difficulties on their own? How can grit be redirected for better learning outcomes?

2. Is the requirement to meet with an advisor enough to help freshmen transition during the first semester in college? What else could the academic advisor have done?
3. What help-seeking behaviors should have been implemented? How are they predictors of success? What are the student's options?
4. In what ways could Jared receive assistance to prevent the threat of losing financial aid to cause him to drop out or stop out? How could his community (lab group, roommate, friends, girlfriend) have been more supportive?
5. What could have been done to avoid exacerbating Jared's medical condition with his hands and arm? How could this have relieved the academic pressure to succeed in anatomy?

Editors' Note: This case study is a hypothetical situation that depicts the type of situation that can happen on college campuses.

REFERENCE

National Student Clearinghouse. (N.d.). The new reality for college students: Earning a bachelor's degree takes 5 to 6 years and students attend multiple institutions. Retrieved on December 15, 2017, from https://nscnews.org/the-new-reality-for-college-students-earning-a-bachelors-degree-takes-5-to-6-years-and-students-attend-multiple-institutions/

TWENTY-EIGHT

Building Walls or Bridges

How to Make Mutually Beneficial Policy Decisions

Sherwood Thompson

The population in the United States is growing, and the cultural identity is changing. According to the U.S. Census Bureau *Quick Facts*, the July 2017 population estimate was 325,719,178. Of that number, the percentage of race population was as shown in Table 28.1.

During the 2016 presidential election, candidate Donald Trump promised that as president, he would build a wall to keep immigrants from illegally crossing the Mexico-U.S. border. On the other hand, presidential candidate Hillary Clinton proposed to build bridges, not walls. This conflict in philosophies characterizes a contentious race in which Trump won the electoral votes and candidate Clinton won the popular vote. Ultimately, Trump won the presidency.

The argument for building a wall to protect the U.S. border with Mexico, which spans about 2,000 miles (Billups, 2015), was based on the

Table 28.1. Percentage of U.S. Population by Race

Whites	76.9%
Black/African Americans	13.3%
American Indians	1.3%
Asians	5.7%
Native Hawaiian/Pacific Islanders	0.2%
Hispanics/Latinos	17.8%
Two or More Races	2.6%

Note: According to the U.S. Census Bureau *Quick Facts*, population estimates, July 1, 2017, by Race (2017). Percentages do not add up to 100% due to rounding and because Hispanics may be of any race.

notion that Mexicans were far too likely to cross over into the United States along the border because the current wall/fence does not offer enough protection. A secondary argument reinforces Trump's stereotypical image of Mexicans. He said after he announced his candidacy for president that Mexico is "sending people that have lots of problems. . . . They're bringing drugs. They're bringing crime. They're rapists. And some, I assume, are good people" (Eleveld, 2015, p. 1). The estimated cost of President Trump's proposed border wall runs anywhere from $8 million to $25 million a mile, according to White House budget director Mick Mulvaney (Dinan, 2017, p. 1).

When candidate Clinton argued that we should be building bridges and not walls, she articulated her belief in developing an alternative form of diplomacy, one that promotes relationship building and a better understanding of our nation's southern neighbors. Candidate Clinton told Luis Megid, a correspondent with Univision, "I think the idea of building walls as an answer to issues that confront our country is just not the right approach. We should be building bridges; we should be building understanding" (Portele, 2016, p. 1).

These opposing arguments were offered to voters in the 2016 presidential election as different plans to protect the border between Mexico and the United States. However, during that debate over illegal immigrants, the candidates and many of their surrogates failed to mention that the "number of Mexican immigrants living in the U.S. illegally has declined by more than 1 million since 2007. In 2014, 5.8 million unauthorized immigrants from Mexico lived in the U.S., down from a peak of 6.9 million in 2007" (Gonzalez-Barrera & Krogstad, 2017, p. 1). In fact, the top five countries of origin for immigrants living illegally in the United States include the following:

- Mexico
- El Salvador
- Guatemala
- Honduras
- The Philippines (Baker and Rytina, 2013)

President Trump has been elected the 45th president of the United States, and he has decided that he will implement his plan for keeping the United States safe from illegal immigrants. Considering both his plan that supports brick-and-mortar construction and his opponent's plan that focused on relationship building, which plan do you believe works best for providing border protection for the United States?

FRAMING THE PROBLEM

Leaders can exhibit many styles and characteristics. Political leadership can be very complex and includes strategic components—one of which is making promises to your constituents. The 2016 presidential election will go down in history as one of the most divisive campaigns in modern times. There were many unusual encounters in the campaign. One of the most fundamental campaign promises came from candidate, now president, Donald Trump. President Trump made a promise to build a wall part of his campaign platform. He also asserted repeatedly that he would get the Mexican government to pay for construction of the wall.

Conducting international border diplomacy, politicians employ different styles and promising practices seeking negotiations with other countries. In the 2016 presidential election, one candidate suggested that the best diplomacy would be to build bridges not walls. However, President Trump insisted that building a wall would keep out the illegals and make the United States safer.

What actually makes a border country safer? Is it bricks and mortar, or is it negotiations around mutual interests? Tough talk or smart diplomacy? How can two border countries maintain a positive relationship as trading partners and friends? These are the challenges that the United States will confront within the coming years.

DISCUSSION QUESTIONS

1. Among the two proposals, which do you think is the best approach to protecting the United States from illegal immigrants crossing over the border?
2. Is one argument more logical than the other for protecting the United States' borders? Why or why not?
3. What are some factors to consider (such as human capital, financial resources, and buy-in from corporate America) that address each proposal, and how feasible would it be, after reviewing the many factors involved with implementing each of these proposals, to accomplish either one of these proposals successfully?
4. Do you favor one of these proposals? If so, which proposal do you favor, and what is your argument for supporting your particular plan?
5. Can you recommend another plan that would accomplish the goal of protecting the borders between the United States and Mexico? How would your proposal work?

REFERENCES

Baker, B., & Rytina, N. (2013). *Estimates of the unauthorized immigrant populations residing in the United States: January 2012*. Homeland Security Office of Immigration Statistics. Retrieved from https://immigration.procon.org/sourcefiles/illegal-immigration-population-2012.pdf

Billups, A. (2015). Illegal immigration: Current length of U.S. Mexico border wall. Retrieved from https://www.newsmax.com/FastFeatures/U-SMexico-border-wall/2015/09/04/id/673637/

Dinan, S. (2017). Trump's border wall is estimated to cost $8 million to $25 million per mile. *Washington Times*. Retrieved from http://www.washingtontimes.com/news/2017/mar/6/white-house-border-wall-could-run-25-million-mile/

Eleveld, K. (2015). Trump: What the village idiot says about the village. *Daily Kos*. Retrieved from http://www.dailykos.com/story/2015/06/16/1393776/-Trump-what-the-village-idiot-says-about-the-village

Gonzalez-Barrera, A., & Krogstad, J. M. (2017). What we know about illegal immigration from Mexico. Pew Research Center. *Fact Tank News in Numbers*. Retrieved from http://www.pewresearch.org/fact-tank/2017/03/02/what-we-know-about-illegal-immigration-from-mexico/

Portele, E. (2016). Hillary tells Univision instead of wall, she will build bridges. *MRC NewsBuster*. Retrieved from http://www.newsbusters.org/blogs/latino/edgard-portela/2016/06/02/hillary-tells-univision-instead-wall-she-will-build-bridges

U.S. Census Bureau. (2017). *Quick Facts*. Retrieved from https://www.census.gov/quickfacts/

TWENTY-NINE

Why and How Should We Talk about Affirmative Action?

M. Kelly Carr

"I'm sick of this. I don't feel particularly privileged," the sweatshirt-clad White woman said from the corner of the class. The class had been discussing their assigned readings, which were pro and con arguments about affirmative action policies in college admissions.

One of the essays defending affirmative action argued that the policies were necessary to alleviate the effects of discrimination against racial minorities and that White applicants did not need special legal protections against discrimination because of their privileged status in American society. Several students expressed their support for this essay, but Beth disagreed strongly.

"My family uses food stamps, and my dad's in jail. I don't have food for lunch today, OK? I gave my lunch to my sister. Where's my privilege?"

Beth went on to explain that she grew up in a low-income, largely White community just outside of the city. In school, Beth explained, she got picked on by other Whites because she was poor, by African Americans because she was poor and White, and by male classmates because she was female. Her voice quivered with anger and grief as she spoke.

Beth had rarely talked in class before now. Over half of the class was African American, and there were several Hispanic students and two international students. Beth had never been a racial minority in a classroom before this semester, and it was intimidating.

Several students had chosen class presentation topics addressing unfair treatment of racial minorities in America, and this frustrated her. She had missed a week of school because her kid sister was sick; her mom couldn't miss work to take care of her, so Beth had to. Since then, Beth had been playing catch-up in all of her classes. Her life didn't feel easier because of her skin color. The class talked about race frequently, and she had grown more and more resentful of the class as the semester dragged on.

As soon as Beth spoke, she felt all eyes upon her. She heard a few people behind her snort. Beth regretted her impulse to speak and worried what the instructor would say—she suspected that Professor Smith was pro–affirmative action and unlikely to be sympathetic. So Beth was surprised when Professor Smith said, "Beth, I really appreciate you sharing your story. I know that took a lot of courage to share something so personal."

Tears stung Beth's eyes, so she looked down at the desk. Please let this moment be over, she thought.

Professor Smith continued, "I think Beth's story illustrates some of the arguments from the essays we read expressing concerns with affirmative action policies. Does anyone remember what the term 'standpoint theory' means?"

The class was still awkwardly silent.

"That's OK. Look through your notes for a minute to refresh your memory," Professor Smith suggested. "Everyone take 10 minutes to find your notes on standpoint theory, then write a paragraph about how two or more elements of your identity or upbringing complicate an understanding of who you are."

Beth felt both annoyed and relieved that Professor Smith had turned the subject away from her story. We've spent so much time in class discussing race, Beth thought. Why stop here?

But as she reviewed her notes and thought about her own life, she realized how standpoint theory related to what had been frustrating her.

Standpoint theory talks about how every person inhabits multiple physical and cultural categories—some seen, some invisible—and those overlapping categories help shape how they experience the world. Race, religion, gender, sexual orientation, physical ability, and socioeconomic status are just a few categories that define us. No one's experience is exactly the same, and no single category defines a person fully. Beth felt like people only saw her as White, not White *and* poor, or White *and* from a broken family, or White *and* a caretaker.

Just White.

After 10 minutes, Professor Smith asked for feedback. Steven, an African-American student, raised his hand. "First, I want to talk about what Beth said. I feel like we're avoiding it."

"Sure, we can," replied Professor Smith. "Just remember the class rules. We are here to discuss ideas, and we use personal stories to exemplify and question those ideas as they relate to the class topic."

"I know. I was gonna say that I agree with her," said Steven. "My experience with standpoint theory is different than hers, but I get the frustration.

My parents are pretty well off. They both have graduate degrees. I get tired of people thinking that I'm poor and raised by a single mom just because I'm Black. I'm an individual. I got into this school because of my test scores, and I worked hard at a competitive school to get them. I earned my spot here, and I hate that people think I didn't. But still . . . my parents had to work twice as hard to get where they are today. So, I guess I'm torn when it comes to affirmative action."

"I earned it, too, Steven," replied Taylor, also an African-American student. "I earned it in a bad school with no AP classes, and I still made good grades. If I got in here because of affirmative action—well, I earned that too because my grandma couldn't even get a job to make a living in this town because she wasn't White. We still take care of her, and ourselves. I think that affirmative action lets me compete with kids from good schools in higher-income areas. Also, I earned it because I can't just dress up and not look Black. White people can dress up and not look poor."

John, a Hispanic student, piped in.

"Steven, maybe it's good that your story breaks a stereotype for other students. Our reading said that the winning legal argument for affirmative action was largely about the educational benefit of a diverse student body. Students can learn from each other's perspectives and experiences. Same with Beth—she's White, but that doesn't automatically get her everything, even if it does give her some advantages, like Taylor said."

Steven replied, "Then why not consider income instead of race? I just can't get on board with making decisions based on race—that feels wrong to me. If the goal is to help people, then wouldn't admitting more people who can't afford it help everyone, without resorting to stereotypes? I don't know. I just think that it should be about merit, not about race."

"But they *already* consider more than just merit in admissions," said Karen, a White student. "I liked the essay that talked about all of the other factors that weigh in—kids whose parents have donated to the school, children of alumni, athletic or musical ability, geographic diversity, even a student's intention to declare a major that the school wants to promote. None of these things count as 'academic merit' in the traditional sense. The Supreme Court says that race can be *one* factor among many admissions criteria. Why should we consider a kid's trombone playing skills, but not his race, when deciding who's the best fit for the school?"

Beth was surprised.

She had regretted her spontaneous comments and thought that everyone would be mad at her. But Steven actually agreed with her. Beth had assumed that any non-White student in the class would automatically support affirmative action policies. And Steven and Taylor disagreed with each other about the value of race and test scores in admissions policies.

Beth didn't agree with Taylor, but she could empathize with Taylor's background and the feeling of never being able to catch a break. She had never thought about being able to hide her poverty in a job interview. John was right, too. Maybe people would learn something about race from Beth's story. But why not avoid race altogether, like Steven said?

Beth left class tired and a bit torn, but she had more perspective on affirmative action than when she came in.

FRAMING THE PROBLEM

Affirmative action is a public policy program developed to lessen some of the material effects of historical discrimination against entire groups of people, usually based on race.

For instance, the results of the 1968 Kerner Report of the National Advisory Commission on Civil Disorders pointed to African-American frustration not just with overt discrimination but also with disproportionate poverty, unemployment, poor education and housing, and systemic police bias. It became clear that abandoning discriminatory practices does not erase the material impact of those practices, and generations continue to suffer from its legacies. Thus, the Kerner Commission recommended programs that carried an immediate impact "in order to close the gap between promise and performance" for all minority groups (Kerner Report, 1968, p. 27).

Affirmative action was one such program. Many businesses, military units, and universities have come to see affirmative action as beneficial to institutional culture and to output. They argue that multiple perspectives enrich decision-making skills for a multicultural society and workforce.

Most people who argue about affirmative action value equality in some sense; but these different senses of equality make a profound difference. For instance, people who are opposed to affirmative action generally think equality means pledging to treat everyone the same, regardless of race. On the other hand, advocates of affirmative action argue that in order to achieve equitable results, we must recognize differences, especially in past treatment.

Another area that sparks differences of opinion about affirmative action is how people operationalize their definitions of race. People who think about race from a historical perspective are more likely to support affirmative action for groups that have been targets of discrimination in the past. People who think of race as skin color alone tend to reject affirmative action policies altogether, because they see race as a meaningless category and race-conscious policies as discriminatory. People who think of race as a cultural factor see race as inhabiting other valuable qualities and shared experiences and see cultural benefits in having a diverse group of people who can learn from each other.

As uncomfortable as conversations about race can be, classroom discussions about the perceptions of affirmative action policies and the benefits of a diverse student body are enormously fruitful. They are not easy, but they fulfill one of the goals of affirmative action in higher education—a robust classroom experience based on diverse perspectives.

DISCUSSION QUESTIONS

1. How would you have felt during the in-class conversation described above?
2. What did these students do well in their class discussion? What could they have done better? Based on your answers, what are some good strategies for talking about race in the classroom? What are some actions to avoid?
3. How well did Professor Smith mediate the conversation? What did she do well? What could she have done better?
4. How does standpoint theory relate to your life?
5. How did each student's thoughts about affirmative action match up with the different understandings of equality and race mentioned in "Framing the Problem"?
6. How do you feel about affirmative action? Do you support or oppose it? Why? Does the context in which it is implemented matter (business, education, military, etc.)? Do you think that fixing the effects of historical discrimination is a better argument for affirmative action, or the benefits of a diverse student body/workforce? Both? Neither?
7. Some people argue, as Steven did, that college affirmative action policies should focus on socioeconomic status instead of racial or ethnic categories. Do you agree or disagree? What would be the advantages and disadvantages of such an approach? What goals of affirmative action does it leave out? What problems does it fix?

Editors' Note: This composite case study reflects the points made in numerous classroom conversations about race and affirmative action over the course of several years. All names are fictional.

REFERENCE

National Advisory Commission on Civil Disorders. (1968). *Report of the National Advisory Commission on Civil Disorders* [The Kerner Report]. New York: Bantam.

THIRTY

Nurturing the Lost Attitudes of Empathy and Compassion in Test-centric Education

Kyung Hee Kim and Sarah M. Nuss

Historical evidence reveals that 1,400 years of cultural obsession with institutionalized, high-stakes standardized testing bears the responsibility for inhibiting Asian innovation (Kim, 2016). In the Sui dynasty (581–618 CE), China first standardized the civil-service testing system, the forerunner of high-stakes standardized tests, to channel ambitious, smart young men to hold power based on their ability, the first example of a standardized meritocracy. Centuries of subscription to this narrow belief in meritocracy allowed a competitive, single-minded focus on academic success to infiltrate every aspect of Asian life. This created exam hell in China, Japan, Korea, Singapore, and Taiwan, which forced students to focus solely on rote memorization, encouraging social apathy (Elman, 2009; Suen & Yu, 2006).

During the 1990s, American politicians, fearing the educational and economic success of Asia, began to focus on high-stakes testing to emulate Asian success. While this focus has cost American taxpayers tens of billions of dollars each year, the real cost of test-centric education is much higher (Kim, 2016). Students' low test scores are often due to structural inequalities beyond their control, starting early in life, such as the number of words exposed to by age three, cultural differences, or lack of family support.

Further, students' test scores, such as ACT and SAT scores, are highly correlated with their parents' income and spending on test preparation, as higher-income families have discretionary funds to pay for test preparation and multiple test-taking sessions (Kim, 2016). Therefore, the claim of meritocracy, deservingness to climb the social ladder to success by fair testing, is used to justify the deservingness of those who scored high and the undeservingness of those who scored low on these standardized tests (Anderson, 2015; Wiederkehr, Bonnot, Krauth-Gruber, & Darnon, 2015). This meritocracy disguises structural inequalities and breeds apathy, blaming low-scoring students for their lack of effort in the United States, while ignoring their possible disadvantages coming into the test (Wiederkehr et al., 2015).

American test-centric education increasingly focuses on students' effort, using such words as *growth mindset* or *grit*. Emphasizing effort is a double-edged sword, as it promotes hard work but convinces students that test scores are the only endeavor worth putting forth effort. If they fail the test, they consider themselves losers early in their lives, diminishing their chances to love doing anything.

This winner-or-loser ethos has traditionally increased students' apathy and competition against others while inhibiting their compassion for others in exam hell. Students who do well on tests believe that those who failed did not put in the effort and therefore do not deserve empathy. This might be a major reason why individuals in exam-hell countries are apathetic toward donating money to charity, volunteering their time, or helping strangers, feeling that those in need did something to deserve their situation. For example, most Asian countries ranked extremely low, especially China ranked 139th among 139 countries in the world, on the World Giving Indexes (Charities Aid Foundation, 2016, 2017). The United States still ranks high on the indexes, but its test-centric education increasingly mirrors Asian exam hell so much that it might eventually become a more apathetic nation.

Empathy is experiencing others' emotions by imagining their perspective and situation. Compassion goes further by taking action to ensure positive outcomes. Empathy and compassion increase creativity, healthy social development, and altruistic behaviors, while decreasing harmful behaviors. However, compared to preceding decades, today's young adults in the United States are more self-centered and show less empathy and compassion, trying less to understand their friends by considering their perspective or having less concerns about people in need (Kim, 2016). Their concern for others outside of their social or campus circles, such as charities, larger social problems, political participation, trust in government, helping the environment, saving energy, and even having a job worthwhile to society, declined (Twenge, Campbell, & Freeman, 2012).

The majority of high school and college students are focused on extrinsic values, such as money, image, and fame, rather than intrinsic values, such as self-acceptance, affiliation, and community (Twenge, 2013; Twenge et al., 2012). Internally, apathy can cause students to lose motivation, become more self-conscious, and have a lesser image of themselves

(Ahmad, 2015). Externally, apathy can do damage outside of the individual, affecting the campus environment, community involvement, social activism, and politics campus-wide, as it can spread quickly throughout peer groups (Ahmad, 2015; Ryan 2011). As we progress generationally toward a more narcissistic society, decreases in empathy can have negative consequences (Twenge, 2013).

RESEARCH-BASED RECOMMENDATIONS

Some universities have reexamined their admissions criteria and made test scores (e.g., ACT/SAT scores) optional, whereas many universities still require test scores. Regardless of the admissions criteria, however, all universities can provide ways to increase empathy among their students, such as service projects. Faculty can encourage students who appear apathetic individually or in small groups to become more involved in service organizations, or even embed service projects into the course syllabus (Loeb, 2001). Faculty can help the students understand that helping others actually helps themselves as it makes the society as a whole better through building relationships and trust.

To encourage students to become empathetic and compassionate, they can learn from tragedies and other current events in national and world news that are caused by insensitivity, cruelty, prejudice, ethnocentrism, xenophobia, and racism. Professors can infuse current events into academic learning through research, discussion, and independent projects to foster empathy and compassion. Universities can also promote service learning by including service involvement as a graduation requirement.

College students themselves can also practice empathy and compassion, through active pursuit, personal development, and relationships. Students can learn from examples of individuals in history who were compassionate and listened to the needs of others. For example (Kim, 2016):

- Mahatma Gandhi reminded the world that nonviolence could be the means to ending conflict.
- Jonas Salk had the courage to invent and administer the polio vaccine to himself and his family before making it public.

Additional active pursuit tips for students to become more empathetic and compassionate (Kim, 2016) include the following:

- Interact with diverse people to learn from their needs and perspectives through meaningful interactions (e.g., extended family, mentors, etc.).

- Get involved in student organizations designed to help others and stand up for others who cannot stand up for themselves.
- Listen and imagine things from others' perspectives without giving solutions to their problems or trying to fix them.
- Acknowledge others' viewpoints and values even when in disagreement.
- Help others move from emotional responses to logical and constructive ones.
- Recognize when others do something that is worthy of recognition and promote it.

Spending time thinking about one's own skills and deficits can also be productive in increasing empathy toward others. Oftentimes, students do not take the time to reflect on themselves and how their behavior can be beneficial for themselves or others. Some specific suggestions for self-reflection (Kim, 2016) include:

- Take control of their future with strong convictions toward their goals, rather than relying on fate.
- Overcome anxiety and fear by gradually exploring, experimenting, takings risks, and making small decisions toward their passion.
- Think of situations where they were hurt and someone showed them empathy, and follow the example.
- Do risky things for bigger purposes, and consider principles and beliefs that are worth taking risks for.
- Consider and understand others' viewpoints, emotions, feelings, attitudes, and motives through exercises like role reversal or role play.
- Read and understand both fiction and nonfiction books that emphasize characters' emotions and develop insights on others' problems and situations.

Relationships are where students can truly express their empathy for others. Listening attentively, appreciating others' feelings, communicating calmly and logically, and being compassionate are all important factors in cultivating productive relationships. From doing small things to make people smile to keeping key information confidential, empathy is critical. Additional suggestions to increase empathetic actions within relationships (Kim, 2016) include the following:

- Interact face-to-face with those they care about rather than only through online technologies.
- Acknowledge others' viewpoints and values even when they disagree.

- Create win-win situations by emphasizing agreement and compromising on disagreement.
- Be compassionate in constructive ways by listening and helping others think positively through negative situations, which include being attentive and letting others finish without interrupting and waiting for them to unfold their thoughts at their own pace.
- Try to think about why others behave in a particular way when experiencing overwhelming feelings.
- Attentively and respectfully listen and assess verbal and nonverbal cues while avoiding interpreting others' body language without verification.
- Be honest, but avoid hurting others' feelings or violating their privacy.

FRAMING THE PROBLEM

Dr. Jones (a fictitious character) has concerns about the impacts of a test-centric education on campus and tries to nurture students' empathy and compassion. In her senior-level English course, students are required to design a service project that would impact a peer on campus. One of her students, Jim, who is in a fraternity, discovered earlier this year that one of his housemates struggles with dysgraphia, a disorder that has impaired his writing skills and ability to perform on tests. Jim has designed a program that includes alternate assessments to assist the housemate. Jim's personal connection with the project has allowed him to be passionate about it and successfully complete it.

DISCUSSION QUESTIONS

1. In what ways has Jim demonstrated empathy or compassion?
2. How can you apply this principle in your own situation?
3. What are other options for the professor to nurture her students' compassion?
4. What types of opportunities to participate in social activism and community outreach are available on your campus?
5. In what ways can your university inspire you to help others?
6. Does one of your professors emphasize empathy and compassion? How so? What have they done to stress the importance of thinking about others?

REFERENCES

Ahmad, S. (2015). Role of socioeconomic status and political participation in construction of apathy among youth. *Journal of Human Behavior in the Social Environment, 25,* 801–9.

Anderson, K. T. (2015). The discursive construction of lower-tracked students: Ideologies of meritocracy and the politics of education. *Education Policy Analysis Archives, 23*(110), 1–30.

Charities Aid Foundation. (2016). *CAF world giving index 2016.* Retrieved from https://www.cafonline.org/about-us/publications/2016-publications/caf -world-giving-index-2016

Charities Aid Foundation. (2017). *CAF world giving index 2017.* Retrieved from https://www.cafonline.org/about-us/publications/2017-publications/caf -world-giving-index-2017

Elman, B. A. (2009). Civil service examinations (Keju). In *Berkshire encyclopedia of China* (pp. 405–410). Great Barrington, MA: Berkshire.

Kim, K. H. (2016). *The creativity challenge: How we can recapture American innovation.* Amherst, NJ: Prometheus.

Loeb, P. R. (2001). Against apathy: Role models for engagement. *Academe, 87*(4), 42–47.

Ryan, M. (2011). Productions of space: Civic participation of young people at university. *British Educational Research Journal, 37,* 1015–31.

Suen, H. K., & Yu, L. (2006). Chronic consequences of high-stakes testing? Lessons from the Chinese civil service exam. *Comparative Education Review, 50*(1), 46–65.

Twenge, J. M. (2013). The evidence for generation me and against generation we. *Emerging Adulthood, 1*(1), 11–16.

Twenge, J. M., Campbell, W. K., & Freeman, E. C. (2012). Generational differences in young adults' life goals, concern for others, and civic orientation, 1966–2009. *Journal of Personality and Social Psychology, 102,* 1045–62.

Wiederkehr, V., Bonnot, V., Krauth-Gruber, S., & Darnon, C. (2015). Belief in school meritocracy as a system-justifying tool for low status students. *Frontiers in Psychology, 6*(1053), 1–10.

THIRTY-ONE

Utilizing Intellectual Diversity to Cultivate Innovation

Kyung Hee Kim and Daria Lorio-Barsten

Creativity is a process of making something unique and useful, and this process can lead to an innovation (Kim, 2016). Something unique requires flexibility of thought and skills to entertain and develop uncommon ideas, which are born out of differing opinions, not consensus. Creativity benefits from cross-pollinating highly diverse perspectives. A diverse group can create distinctive ideas, drawing on a variety of experiences and ideas from different backgrounds, thoughts, views, and skills. This chapter defines intellectual diversity, considers the role of neurodiversity, and makes recommendations for universities as well as students to increase intellectual diversity.

Discussions regarding diversity on campus generally have focused on racial diversity.

As the population of the United States continues to become more heterogeneous, universities must strive to meet the needs of a more racially diverse society. Frequent racially diverse interactions improve students' learning outcomes, intellectual engagement, leadership skills, and psychological well-being, and those who experience dissonance from these interactions develop complex thought processes and critical-thinking skills (Pascarella et al., 2014).

To promote intellectual and social student growth, universities must look beyond racial diversity and also strive for intellectual diversity. Intellectual diversity is a multiplicity of ideas, ideologies, philosophies, views, and other perspectives and is the main contributor to creativity and innovation. Remarkable ideas are necessary to go beyond current knowledge and achieve innovation. These ideas flourish in the presence of diverse intellectual perspectives, where conformity and the status quo are challenged. Notable innovators in history thought and behaved differently from others and therefore were often misunderstood or seen as troublemakers.

Some notable innovators with diverse intellectual perspectives include (Kim, 2016):

- Albert Einstein, who was the only graduate in his department who could not find a job for two years after graduation because none of his professors would write a letter of recommendation for him, as he thought and behaved differently from them.
- Georgia O'Keefe, who was viewed negatively by the proper southern girls after her family moved from Wisconsin to Virginia. She was strong and independent, and as an adult, many in the male-dominated art world viewed her negatively because she, as a pioneering female artist, did not conform to gender norms.
- Nelson Mandela was viewed negatively when he ran away from his arranged marriage, refusing to conform to his tribe's tradition; and as an adult, he was viewed negatively by many in the White-dominated nation of South Africa because he was a Black man who refused to stay in his place.

Einstein, O'Keefe, and Mandela shared the nonconforming, defiant, and even rebellious attitude, which enabled their ideas to differ from the majority and become innovators.

Further, intellectual diversity includes neurodiversity, a strength-based view of intellectual differences, which shifts away from a deficit-based view that individuals with developmental or mental disorders, such as autism, dyslexia, attention deficit hyperactivity disorder, and intellectual disabilities, are deficient rather than different (Griffin & Pollak, 2009). Rather than seeing abnormalities, neurodiversity celebrates differences in development.

Neurodiverse individuals are often misunderstood or perceived negatively due to their different ideas or behaviors from the majority, especially in social settings. However, neurodiverse individuals who have adopted the strength-based view exhibit stronger academic self-esteem and set greater career goals than those with the deficit-based view (Griffin & Pollak, 2009). Moreover, because the foundation of creative thinking is expertise in a specific area, neurodiverse individuals are poised to leverage their unique skills to gain mastery and become innovators (Kim, 2016).

As the number of neurodiverse individuals is growing, colleges, workplaces, and communities encounter more neurodiverse individuals. Employers, particularly in the area of technology, have embraced the value of adding neurodiverse individuals to their companies. Several companies, such as Microsoft, Hewlett Packard, and Ford, are recruiting neurodiverse employees and have even changed their human resources procedures to do so (Austin & Pisano, 2017). Employment of neurodiverse individuals has led managers to reach the individual talents of various employees (Austin & Pisano, 2017).

RESEARCH-BASED RECOMMENDATIONS

Universities must prepare graduates for a diverse society, including neurodiversity, by cultivating ranges of viewpoints and essential competencies like critical-thinking skills. Universities must help students accept and view their diversities as strengths, use their uniqueness to fulfill their dreams, and provide outlets for communicating students' challenges and successes. Although many educators saw only the negative aspects of the aforementioned innovators' intellectual diversities, other individuals saw these innovators' strengths, uniqueness, and potentials by cultivating creative climates to enhance their intellectual diversities and encourage positive aspects of their attitudes (Kim, 2016).

Creativity has the power to transform the good into the best, and every student, no matter their background or learning style, deserves the opportunity that creativity brings. The following sections discuss how students can nurture their intellectual diversity by, first, knowing their own identity; second, building their craft; and third, becoming a change agent for creativity (Kim, 2016).

1. Know and Express Oneself

Enhancing intellectual diversity starts with students knowing themselves and becoming comfortable with being an intellectual minority. They must take responsibility for their own life and not let anyone dictate their worth. The process of identifying their uniqueness can begin as simply as, first, naming a favorite thing, person, hobby, song, motto, or philosophy by which they live; second, identifying these differences as forms of diversity; and third, celebrating how their diversity enriches their own and others' lives. They can recognize what inspires them, while rejecting the expectations of others of what their lives *should* be, by developing their own beliefs through critically thinking about their world and:

- Test socially accepted facts, and seek proof through experimentation, discovery, or observation.
- Evaluate the reliability and validity of information from the media, and write to the media to correct mistakes.

- Question popular and common beliefs, and be willing to hold unpopular views on issues, especially when others are afraid to.
- Challenge others' opinions, expectations, beliefs, and stereotypes respectfully, and break the rules responsibly.

Being an intellectual minority can be uncomfortable. Students must develop resilience and willingness to reject conformity, resist convention, and overcome the fear of rejection to reach their own potential. Uncomfortable experiences may include being mocked or teased for being unusual and showing their desires; however, they should be encouraged to continue forward with their desires and interests.

Students may also feel that society confines them in certain forms of expression and gender roles, but they should, instead, be encouraged to be free to express themselves as they want to, whether via sexuality, profession, language, religion, or how they live. Students must become comfortable with unpopular ideas and find ways to respectfully express them, despite social pressures. They can start practicing expressing themselves by:

- Discussing their needs or desires, and advocating for their choices.
- Asking others for assistance when needed.
- Finding something small to firmly and politely say "no" to.
- Joining groups that are unfamiliar, and consciously noticing when they are following others, and deciding to do otherwise.

2. Build the Craft

Students must build their individual strengths by focusing on something they excel in and establishing themselves as an authority over it. By focusing on a specialty, students can show who they truly are to the world, instead of comparing themselves to other successful people and wishing they had what they have. Students can develop something they are passionate about and align their actions with that passion by:

- Finding their purpose, and focusing on helping others; money will follow.
- Creating their own path by reigniting the passion behind their mission, purpose, and ultimate goal; and evaluating whether each task will get them closer to their goal.
- Developing a new concept, approach, or product by:

  o Thinking dramatically differently from others and breaking away from conventional ways of thinking.
  o Overcoming mental barriers, such as rigid rules about what is allowed and what works.

There are no shortcuts in innovation. Only active patience is rewarded. Students must take time and work on their skills and craft. They should appreciate their own and others' strengths to develop their own styles. While leaving room for mistakes and errors, they should constantly assess their own work to improve it for its usefulness first and then focus on making their work different for its uniqueness. They must learn, understand, and conform to the existing rules or constraints in a system or tradition first, and then challenge or change them within the system or the tradition.

3. Become a Change Agent

Students must seek visibility and cross-pollination to increase opportunities for innovation through networking, collaboration, and win-win competition. They must seek suggestions and guidance from others while remaining free to choose what to do with the suggestions. They must create allies by finding others who share and believe in similar views, and surround themselves with the right people to support their mission and goals. They must evaluate current systems in place; develop defiance against inconsistent or unjust rules, norms, or values; and stand up for their beliefs and for people who share them. They must speak up for the victims of bullies and against inequality and connect with current debates on inequality and social justice in the community.

To become change agents, students can:

- Consider multiple angles to a situation and different viewpoints by engaging in complex, varied, and expressive dialogues and debates.
- Encourage others to disagree with them, listen to others' arguments, and explain their own positions.
- Take a controversial issue that they feel strongly about, write two essays (one to defend their opinion and one to oppose it) using factual evidence or citations, and then present to an audience or share with others for feedback.
- Learn how to compromise, negotiate, and work with someone who has different skills.
- Pick battles wisely to fight for issues that matter the most, and strategically break unjust or wrong rules.

FRAMING THE PROBLEM

Eddie (a hypothetical person) has autism. One of Eddie's assignments in class included working on a group project that accounted for a quarter of his final grade. He was excited to work on the project because he was confident in his knowledge of the content. During the group meetings, he was quick to share everything he knew about the topic and pointed out anytime anyone else within the group made a mistake or misunderstood the content. His group members did not appear to share his enthusiasm. Eddie noticed that his group members started to interrupt him frequently and directed questions only to each other and never to him.

DISCUSSION QUESTIONS

1. How will current group dynamics impact the quality of the final project?
2. What skills do all group members need to move forward in a more effective manner?
3. How can Eddie work better in a group, come to know his uniqueness, continue to build his craft, and become a change agent for creativity?
4. If you were one of Eddie's group members, how would you foster intellectual diversity in your group?
5. How does your campus foster an accepting and supportive learning community to increase intellectual diversity? What are the responsibilities of professors as well as students to promote such a community?
6. Think of the last time you collaborated with others. How did your group support or create barriers for intellectual diversity? What would you do differently?

REFERENCES

Austin, R. D., & Pisano, G. P. (2017). Neurodiversity as a competitive advantage. *Harvard Business Review, 3*. Retrieved from https://hbr.org/2017/05/neuro diversity-as-a-competitive-advantage

Griffin, E., & Pollak, D. (2009). Student experiences of neurodiversity in higher education: Insights from the BRAINHE project. *Dyslexia, 15*, 23–41. doi:10.1002/dys.383

Kim, K. H. (2016). *The creativity challenge: How we can recapture American innovation.* Amherst, NY: Prometheus.

Pascarella, E. T., Martin, G. L., Hanson, J. M., Trolian, T. L., Gillig, B., & Blaich, C. (2014). Effects of diversity experiences on critical thinking skills over 4 years of college. *Journal of College Student Development, 55*(1), 86–92. doi:10.1353/csd.2014.0009

THIRTY-TWO

Outnumbered

Is Conservatism Truly under Attack on College Campuses?

Willie R. Tubbs

One day, early in my career as a college instructor, mistakes on my part led to my "Introduction to Writing for Mass Media" being derailed. The lecture that day was about something important, but not all that explosive. I can't remember if I was covering active voice, misplaced modifiers, or the ins and outs of the comma. I share this mainly to establish that I was not covering a political topic.

I was covering about as politically neutral a topic as can be imagined.

About two-thirds of the way through this 50-minute section, a young man raised his hand. I assumed he needed me to restate something, but I was wrong. The student told me he understood that I wouldn't like his opinion, because he could tell I was "a bleeding-heart liberal" professor, but he didn't understand why people criticized Fox News. He also wondered why I wouldn't just tell everyone upfront what my political leanings were.

Forget coming out of left field, this student had come from outside the city limits in which the field was located. A combination of shock and being a greenhorn led me to stumble through a defense of myself. I think I managed to convey that I was politically moderate, registered as an independent, and unsure how any of this related to grammar.

The student was not convinced.

"I'm just saying, man. My dad and I were discussing this the other day, and he said most professors are just liberals. You know, it's all indoctrination."

I am far better equipped to handle these types of situations today. While I've not had any other students bring the topic up in so strange a manner, or at such an odd time, I have occasionally had students ask about liberal biases in the classroom. As most of my classes are predicated on instilling the journalistic standard of objectivity, I usually defuse the situation by saying, "Grammar is apolitical. Conservative, liberal, or apathetic, we all need to know how to spell."

If it's a reporting class, I say, "Just like good journalists strive to remove biases from their final products, so, too, do I strive to not infuse my politics into my instruction."

These encounters with conservative students are usually brief, and I've never had anyone shout me down. Even the student who interrupted my class was guilty of nothing more than odd timing. Still, the episode bears some consideration.

My brief exchange speaks to two factors, both of which relate to diversity of thought on campus.

First, I find myself questioning the effectiveness of my approach in fostering a diverse sphere of ideas on campus. My nonengagement system tends to keep the peace, but it doesn't address the student's concern head on.

Second, the episode speaks to a growing issue across academia. Specifically, many conservative students believe that they exist in a sea of hard-left professors and students and that their political beliefs are under attack. While my gut reaction is, "It's not as bad as all that," it's necessary to ponder conservative students' concerns.

FRAMING THE PROBLEM

The problems in my mini-drama were twofold. Pedagogically, instructors and classmates must determine how, or if, they will deal with a student expressing an opinion in class. When this expression is to the detriment of the class, most professors agree to not go down the rabbit hole.

But the nonengagement approach is not universally useful. Political science professors would do a disservice to their students if they refused to engage political discourse. But where is the line drawn? At which point, or under which class description, do we cross from the appropriate to inappropriate time to engage in political debate?

The latter is a far more complex and unique problem inasmuch as it might not even be a problem. In my brief episode of being accused of being a hard-left liberal, my student had nothing to fear. I do not have an anticonservative lean, and even if I did, I'd never let that affect the way I graded a conservative student's work.

But what about countless other students with conservative leanings at other schools? Do they have a case?

Anyone who has followed the news over the past several years knows there is some anecdotal evidence to suggest that there are some universities at which there are at least a few people who seek to suppress or drown out conservative voices. The issue, then, isn't determining if some conservative students have been treated poorly, somewhere—they have, and I condemn any professor or student group that would seek to intimidate or abuse others. Rather, the issue is to determine if what we see in the media is representative of a trend or of troubling outliers.

Attempts to suppress speech on campuses were launched by left-leaning student groups. In that year, FIRE tracked 29 attempts to prevent guest speakers from presenting on campus. Twenty-four of these attempts were made by left-leaning groups compared to four attempts by right-leaning groups. The 29th attempt was, at least in terms of American politics, neither left- nor right-oriented. The outlier involved a group of Chinese students at the University of California–San Diego who wished to deplatform the Dalai Lama due to his advocacy for a free Tibet (https://www.thefire.org/resources/disinvitation-database).

The groups who sought to silence political opposition had mixed results. The move to deplatform the Dalai Lama, for example, failed. So, too, did an attempt by students to prevent conservative firebrand Milo Yiannopoulos from speaking at the University of New Mexico, although he was prevented from speaking at Cal–Berkeley after violent protests erupted before a national television audience. Conservative comedian and talk show host Gavin McInnes was disinvited from both DePaul and NYU. Ben Shapiro, another conservative talk show host, was deplatformed at Marquette. Political scientist Charles Murray received the heckler's veto plus violence at private Middlebury College and subsequently had his invitation to speak at Assumption College revoked due to security concerns (https://www.thefire.org/resources/disinvitation-database).

Do efforts to deplatform speakers at 20-odd universities constitute an all-out assault on conservatism? The National Center for Educational Statistics reports there are 6,760 Title IV colleges and universities in the United States and its territories (Ginder, Kelly-Reid, & Mann, 2017). A Title IV school is defined as one that processes federal financial aid. That means that about 0.002958% of colleges in the United States were home to an attempted or successful deplatforming in 2017. While I would be troubled if even one deplatforming occurred, these numbers hardly constitute proof of widespread anticonservativism.

This is not to say that there have not been profound attacks on free expression. From 2015 to 2017, there have been several instances that many conservatives, students and nonstudents alike, point to as evidence of anticonservative bias. Without relitigating each episode, let's run down the events:

- In 2015, a professor at the University of Missouri was caught on camera asking for "some muscle" to remove a journalist from among students gathered for a rally. The professor was eventually fired. (Kolowich, Read, and Thomason, 2016)
- In February 2017, the University of California–Berkeley campus erupted in violence when Yiannopoulos attempted to speak. (Park and Lah, 2017)
- In 2017, Evergreen State College students requested that all White people voluntarily leave campus for a day. When this request was not honored, a group of students effectively took over the school, shouting down at least one professor and briefly occupying the president's office. (Hartcollis, 2017)

There are other lesser examples, but I have heard these three most frequently. While I was troubled by each of these events, only one was related directly to conservatism, and even Yiannopoulos would say he exists on the outskirts of the right. And, it must be noted, Yiannopoulos was eventually allowed to speak at Berkeley (Quintana, 2017).

Evergreen State College serves as a great example of a tendency people on the left and right have to treat conservatism and Whiteness as interchangeable. In the case of the University of Missouri, the student journalist the professor had removed identifies as a liberal, and the professor was terminated for her actions. Missouri stands not as an example of an attack on conservatism, but as an example of people conflating freedom of the press with conservatism.

Not that there isn't real cause for concern in the area of freedom of expression. At the time of this writing, FIRE identifies 125 schools as "code red" institutions, the group's designation for universities at which expression is under attack. This does not mean that 125 universities have policies in place that threaten conservatism, though; only that expression in general is under threat. On its website, FIRE defines a "red light" university as once that "has at least one policy that both clearly and substantially restricts freedom of speech. A 'clear' restriction is one that unambiguously infringes on what is or should be protected expression."

The true problem, I believe, is that conservative students know that, at least at state schools, a large portion of their professors tend to lean liberal. That is quantifiably true, but is it truly a problem? Are conservative students under threat? While conservatism might not dominate the political leanings of faculty at state schools, there are few campuses in the United States at which conservative groups do not exist. And, at least to an extent, some student-led conservative groups have been active and effective in political matters. For example, as described by Nathan R. Todd, Elizabeth A. McConnell, Charlynn A. Odahl-Ruan, and Jaclyn D.

Houston-Kolnik in 2016, conservative Christian groups had an impact in the debate over gay marriage.

Simple mathematics and common sense dictate that it is unlikely to ever be a 50–50 split, or even representative split, among political ideologies. The number of liberals will be what it will be. Same for conservative, libertarian, etc. The goal, I've always thought, was to allow for all ideas to be represented, debated, debunked, etc. But it is hard to totally discount the conservative students in the face of stark, albeit statistically rare, examples of liberal overreach.

Perhaps the challenge is to assure that the aforementioned troubling outliers, the deplatforming efforts and violent outburst in which people were targeted for their political beliefs, remain just that—outliers.

DISCUSSION QUESTIONS

1. Put yourself in the place of the instructor. How would you address a student who asks an unrelated political question? Is nonengagement the correct response? How would you respond to a student who felt his or her conservative beliefs were being looked down upon?
2. Do conservative students have a point? Is there an intentional or unintentional marginalization of conservative voices on campuses?
3. Are instances like those at Evergreen State College, Missouri, and Berkeley or the 24 deplatforming efforts outliers or indicative of a broader problem of attacks on free speech and/or conservatism at colleges and universities the nation over?
4. Are Whiteness and conservatism interchangeable?
5. Does a professor have the right to espouse liberal views to students during a class? Does a professor have the right to espouse conservative views to students during a class?

REFERENCES

Ginder, S. A., Kelly-Reid, J. E., & Mann, F. B. (2017). *Postsecondary institutions and cost of attendance in 2016–17; degrees and other awards conferred, 2015–16; and 12-month enrollment, 2015–16.* U.S. Department of Education, Integrated Postsecondary Education Data System, & Institute of Education Sciences National Center for Education Statistics. Retrieved from https://nces.ed.gov/pubs2017/2017078.pdf

Foundation for Individual Rights in Education. Disinvitation attempts. Retrieved from https://www.thefire.org/resources/disinvitation-database/

Foundation for Individual Rights in Education. Spotlight database and activism portal. Retrieved from https://www.thefire.org/spotlight/

Hartcollis, A. (2017, June 16). A campus argument goes viral: Now the college is under siege. *New York Times*. Retrieved from https://www.nytimes.com/2017/06/16/us/evergreen-state-protests.html

Kolowich, S., Read, B., & Thomason, A. (2016, February 26). 10 revealing details in the Melissa Click investigation. *Chronicle of Higher Education*. Retrieved from https://www.chronicle.com/article/10-Revealing-Details-in-the/235502

Park, M., & Lah, K. (2017, February 2). Berkeley protests of Yiannopoulos caused $100,000 in damage. CNN website. Retrieved from https://www.cnn.com/2017/02/01/us/milo-yiannopoulos-berkeley/index.html

Quintana, C. (2017, September 22). As "Free Speech Week" crumbled, Berkeley braced for . . . something. *Chronicle of Higher Education*. Retrieved from https://www.chronicle.com/article/As-Free-Speech-Week-/241280

Todd, N. R., McConnell, E. A., Odahl-Ruan, C. A., & Houston-Kolnik, J. D. (2016). Christian campus-ministry groups at public universities and opposition to same-sex marriage. *Psychology of Religion and Spirituality, 9*(4), 412–22.

THIRTY-THREE

Affirmative Action

Where Are My Brothers and Sisters?

Adriel A. Hilton, Errick D. Farmer, and Antoine Lovell

John was born and raised in the South in a predominately African-American community. Throughout his primary and secondary school years, he attended predominately African-American schools. He felt very comfortable within and outside this community.

After high school, he considered several college options. He knew his family would want him to attend a college they attended, but he had different thoughts. He wanted to try something different from his parents, and different is just what he did.

John enrolled in a prestigious, predominantly White institution, and as he moved around campus he was very glad to see many other African-American students. After all, he grew up in this type of environment. He had thoughts about attending one of the historically Black colleges and universities (HBCUs), but after seeing other African Americans on campus, near the union and café, he felt as if he had made the right decision.

He could not wait for classes to start the following week, and he was very excited about this new adventure. As he attended his first class, he arrived early and found a seat toward the front of class, just as he had always done in high school. As the professor began class, he decided to look around to see some of his classmates. He saw no one who looked like him. He quickly thought to himself, "I'm all alone. Where are my brothers and sisters?" He knew he was at a predominantly White institution (PWI), and maybe this was expected, but he thought he would see more persons such as himself.

Affirmative action policies often focus on employment and education. In institutions of higher education, affirmative action refers to admission policies that provide equal access to education for those groups that have been historically excluded or underrepresented, such as women and minorities (National Conference of State Legislatures, 2014).

While initially John did not believe in affirmative action and felt that individual merit and ability should be the basis of their opportunity, he no longer felt that way. He began to question why he decided to attend this school and why he was not better informed about his decision. As he began to do more research, he found some unsettling information.

A study from the University of Washington in 2013 found that minority students have a harder time getting accepted to public research universities in states that have banned affirmative action (Blume & Long, 2014). Researchers looked at the effect race had on admissions and saw a 23 percentage point drop in the chance of admission for minority students in states with bans, compared with a 1 percentage point drop in other states, relative to nonminority students.

California, Washington, Michigan, Nebraska, Arizona, and Oklahoma all passed bans through voter referenda. In Florida, Governor Jeb Bush issued an executive order creating the ban. And in New Hampshire, the legislature passed a bill banning the consideration of race (Potter, 2014). Together, these eight states educate 29% of all U.S. high school students.

To say the least, John was very disappointed. The Civil Rights Act is a little over 50 years old, and already there have been challenges to affirmative action. Although he decided that leaving this PWI would not make anything better, he grappled with lingering questions about equity and representation on college campuses.

FRAMING THE PROBLEM

John is an African-American male, and after graduation, he enrolled in a prestigious predominately White institution. Upon entering his first class, John quickly noticed he was the only African American in class. He also learned that the school he decided to attend did not employ affirmative action for admission decisions. These factors have impacted how John feels about his institutional choice.

DISCUSSION QUESTIONS

1. Do you think affirmative action is still needed in the college admissions process? Why or why not?
2. If you think it is not now needed, do you think it was needed when it was first implemented years ago?

3. Based upon the facts in the case, should the university provide information regarding affirmative action on its admissions website? Why or why not?
4. Research shows that affirmative action hurts the admissions process for minorities. What diversity strategies should universities use to promote diversity on campus?
5. What can universities do to better address these issues on their campuses?

Editors' Note: This hypothetical situation represents a real-world problem in academe.

REFERENCES

Blume, G. H., & Long, M. C. (2014). Changes in levels of affirmative action in college admissions in response to statewide bans and judicial rulings. *Educational Evaluation and Policy Analysis, 2,* 228–52.

National Conference of State Legislatures. (2014, February 7). Affirmative action. Retrieved May 15, 2017, from http://www.ncsl.org/research/education/affirmative-action-overview.aspx

Potter, H. (2014, June 26). What can we learn from states that ban affirmative action. Retrieved May 15, 2017, from https://tcf.org/content/commentary/what-can-we-learn-from-states-that-ban-affirmative-action/

THIRTY-FOUR

Welcome, Not Celebrated

Are Christian Campuses Truly Inclusive for Sexually Diverse Students?

Willie R. Tubbs

The following story is a composite of several different conversations I had at my undergraduate alma mater, Louisiana College.

LC, a small Baptist liberal arts school in Pineville, holds a dear place in my heart, and I can assure you that the place is not hate filled. However, it is filled with traditionalist values, a fact that makes the school's interaction with LGBT students nothing short of fascinating.

In 2009, I returned to my alma mater and took a job as sports information director. My duties took me all over campus and afforded me the chance to get to know many students, those inside and outside the athletics family. In my four years at LC, I was treated to many pleasant conversations about life and faith with students.

Students at Louisiana College come from diverse backgrounds, which makes it all the stranger how students react when they learn of LGBT persons attending the school.

Given the poor state of relations between LGBT persons and conservative Christians, you might assume that the reaction to news of someone expressing a nontraditional sexuality would be anguish. In reality, people at LC were mostly cordial, or at least impassive, although there were always a few voices of extreme judgment. The students at Louisiana College were then and are now well meaning and unlikely to condemn anyone to hell. While there were some students who would shun those who are different, I was never aware of any student being alienated from most of his or her classmates.

At an institutional level, things weren't quite so simple. As a matter of policy, it was and still is against the rules to advocate homosexuality on campus. The good news for LGBT students is that Louisiana College does not have a rule that punishes students for being gay or lesbian. This wasn't always the case. There was a time when identifying as gay or lesbian was grounds for official sanction.

That all changed during the presidency of Barack Obama.

Society as a whole was evolving, but President Obama also pushed for schools to officially stand against discrimination based on sexuality or risk losing federal funding. President Obama was hardly reinventing the system. Title IX regulations have long held such standards. However, with the emergence of the right to same-sex marriage, momentum and federal mandates were on the side of LGBT students.

Even at private schools, federal funding has a way of getting people's attention. During the Obama administration, Christian schools began adding in language to their policies that made it clear that no student or potential student was unwelcome because of their sexuality.

Louisiana College is funded jointly by donors, the Louisiana Baptist Convention, and tuition. The federal government might not have any authority over the first two groups, but most students at Louisiana College were on some form of federal aid. Were Louisiana College, or virtually any other school for that matter, to lose the ability to steer students to federally backed grants and scholarships, tough economic times if not closure would soon follow. To that end, as of today, Louisiana College maintains a policy that welcomes a diverse student body.

Despite this, Campus Pride, a nonprofit organization geared toward fostering safer college environments for LGBT students, includes Louisiana College on its "List of Shame." At present, Campus Pride lists 139 colleges and universities that the organization deems "unsafe" for LGBT students.

For me, who went to Louisiana College when it was possible for LGBT students to be punished just for "being" gay, it is strange to see the school associated with anti-LGBT sentiment when, in reality, the school has adopted its most liberal stance on sexuality.

However, this is a nuanced issue, and Campus Pride has a case. While the federal government can compel, some might argue coerce, private schools into welcoming sexually diverse students, the schools enjoy the freedom, ironically, to restrict speech.

Louisiana College is one of many schools that applied for and received a Title IX waiver, which allows the school to maintain some of its anti-LGBT policies without penalty. In the case of Louisiana College, this exemption was granted in a July 31, 2015, letter from Catherine E. Lhamon, assistant secretary for civil rights, U.S. Department of Education, under President Obama (https://www.campuspride.org/wp-content/uploads/louisiana-college-response-07312015.pdf).

The exemption is broad. While the school is required to be officially welcoming to people of all walks of life, Louisiana College retains the right to restrict students from advocating for pro-LGBT causes or practicing their sexuality in public. It must be added that the restriction on physical intimacy is mostly in line with the rules the school has for heterosexual students, who are also forbidden from public displays of affection.

On its website, Campus Pride points to this exemption as justification for the school's inclusion on the "List of Shame" (www.campuspride. org/shamelist): "Louisiana College has qualified for the Shame List because it holds an exemption to Title IX, allowing the college to discriminate against its students on the basis of sexual orientation, gender identity, marital status, pregnancy or receipt of abortion while still receiving Federal funds." In short, the school welcomes LGBT students but forbids them or their allies from defending their lifestyle or advocating for policies the school deems un-Christian. Those who force the issue are subject to severe academic penalty, including expulsion.

Even in the days prior to the more inclusive language, I never met a student, nor heard of a student, who was expelled from LC for her or his sexuality. The expulsions with which I am familiar were the result of doctrinal disagreement (which might warrant its own case study in future), drinking, drugs, or arrests. The school is definitely not willing to change its stance on homosexuality as a sin, but the LC does welcome all and pray for all, even if the school is still coming to terms with a modern society.

FRAMING THE PROBLEM

Is it possible to abhor someone's lifestyle yet still welcome that person on a campus?

Many private schools in the United States argue that it is. Over the past few years, in the face of federal pressure, many private Christian schools have softened their stance on LGBT matters. But can LGBT persons ever be truly welcome at private schools that embrace a traditional approach to Christianity? Can a school claim to be inclusive while still arguing that a person's lifestyle is sinful?

LGBT rights on private Christian campuses is a complicated issue, but the problem boils down to three broad conundrums. First, can Christian schools that adhere to a traditional, conservative application of doctrine ever satisfy the tenets of inclusion of LGBT people? Second, how much oversight should the federal government have over private schools? Third, would stripping noncompliant Christian schools of their ability to process federal financial aid be an equitable solution? Put another way, should non-LGBT students who wish to attend a traditional, Christian institute of higher education be afforded less financial aid because of their religious beliefs?

Proponents of Christian schools' right to govern expression on their campuses largely center their argument around religious liberty. If a school does not allow for the mistreatment of gay students, the school has provided protection. Should the school be forced to abandon its religious convictions as well? It is worth noting that at Louisiana College, lots of non-LGBT advocacy can get a student in trouble as well.

It will likely surprise no one to learn that the school is pro-life, but there have been times when students and staff have run afoul of the Louisiana College handbook for their interpretation of Scripture. Schools rooted in traditional conceptions of family and sexuality hold views that might run against popular sentiment, but it has long been established that these institutions are free to exercise their beliefs.

But there is another level to this problem: the students of private colleges. If Title IX exemptions are removed and schools are forced to either adapt or lose funding, would the punishment be meted out to the intended target? In spirit, an attempt to force Christian schools to allow for the open advocacy of LGBT rights would be aimed at the leaders of the school, those men and women who created the policies.

But what about the students who wish to attend a more traditional school? Is it the government's place to deny money to students to attend the college of their choice? Remember, the loans and federal funds don't go to the school directly, but to students who use the money to pay tuition to the school. The school isn't saddled with thousands in loan debt; the student is. Thus, would it be encroaching on the students' rights if you tell them they cannot attend a religious school because it has controversial stances? What about non-Christian private schools? Would you be comfortable stripping away federal funding from students at hard-left private schools for not welcoming traditional Christian students?

It occurs to me that in discussing the reality of life on campus for LGBT people at Christian schools, we should really be looking off campus. The issue is as much about a federal government that allows concessions to private religious schools as it is about schools that put their doctrine to practice in higher education.

But the issue is not as simple as forcing religious schools to comply or take away funding, or for the government to stay out of religious affairs altogether and simply allocate funds for students to use anywhere and in any way.

This might seem at first like the same-sex wedding cake issue come to campus, but this is a much more complicated matter. When Christian bakers refuse service to gay couples on religious grounds, the issue is far

more clear cut. Does a business owner's religious belief trump antidis-
crimination laws?

When LGBT students are granted admission to conservative Christian
colleges but are then saddled with the same speech restrictions as non-
LGBT students, the situation becomes murkier. The question becomes,
does a student's right to expression trump a private school's right to create universal regulations on its campus?

DISCUSSION QUESTIONS

1. Are Christian schools right, not to be mistaken within their rights, to
   ask for Title IX exemptions from the federal government?
2. Is the federal government right to allow Title IX exemptions?
3. Can you envision a policy under which a school can both be truly welcoming to LGBT people and against the practice of homosexuality?
4. Pretend you are a decision maker in the federal government. How
   would you balance religious freedom with the rights of all on private campuses?
5. How much oversight should the federal government exert over
   college students' religious beliefs? Should the federal government
   limit funds to students who wish to attend schools with Title IX
   exemptions?
6. Would it be proper for the federal government to deny federal
   funding for all private schools, be they religious or secular, thereby
   eliminating the ability of most smaller private schools to operate? Or
   is it better for the federal government to continue to fund all private
   schools and use the threat of stripping said funds as a means to inspire policy changes?

REFERENCES

Campus Pride. *List of shame*. Retrieved from www.campuspride.org/shamelist
Lhamon, C. E. (2015, July 31). *Letter to Louisiana College president*. Retrieved
    from https://www.campuspride.org/wp-content/uploads/louisiana-college
    -response-07312015.pdf

UNIT 4
STUDENT ORGANIZATIONS

THIRTY-FIVE

First-Generation College Students

Our Group Is the Best!

Eleni Oikonomidoy

Maria and Stephan are mentors in a program that serves first-generation college students. On this particular day, they are talking about their observations of their program's successes and failures. As they share the multiple successful stories that they have either observed or have heard from their students, Maria brings up a point that Stephan had not thought about. She shares her concern with what she refers to as the territorial behavior of their students.

"Stephan, one of the issues that I am puzzled with is the tension that I sense between membership to our program and other programs. I hear that there is some 'hidden' competition and that students are told to choose a side," she said.

Stephan is surprised to hear about this at first. But then, after giving it some thought, he agrees that there is some truth to the statement. He recalls overhearing a student a few days ago telling another, "Hey man, you have to pick your side. You can't be here and there. We are rivals and our program means the world to us."

At the time, he thought this was just a joke. But now that he is thinking about it, he is not so sure.

Maria shares that she believes that having a program to identify with is of great importance to first-generation college students who, oftentimes, find the campus environment alien. She shares her pride in the cultivation of trusting relationships among members of her program. But she doesn't want this reality to overshadow the experiences of her students and prevent them from engaging with others.

She is puzzled by the exclusionary character of group membership and of the potential negative impact that it has on students' social engagement on campus. Prior to raising this issue to the program coordinator, she invites Stephan to an informal exploration of this reality.

Maria is a graduate student who has taken multiple research classes. She decides to practice her research skills by surveying students in the program. Stephan, who is also a graduate student, agrees to help code-sign and execute the mini–research project. Given that they take into consideration how their positions as mentors may influence students' responses, they decide to talk to students who are not their mentees over the next month.

They are surprised with the results.

Their suspicion that students' identification with the program resulted in animosity toward other programs was confirmed. Some of the representative comments that they heard included: "While we talk to those from similar programs, we stick to our own group." "Yes, of course, I talk to others. My friends, though, are those who are close to me and go to the same program. These are my sisters. We have so much in common." "Just the other day, my friend asked me to go to an event that they put together. Not only I did not want to go; I also told my friend to stay put and not betray his loyalty to us. Our group has to stay together, you know?" "I don't know anyone from another group on campus. I am fine staying close to home. My own program. This is my family on campus."

Upon completion of their informal study, Maria and Stephan pondered whether the same was true for all students who belonged to the multiple programs and organizations on campus. Were all efforts to provide spaces for people to belong leading to exclusion and segregation? What mechanisms should be in place to promote sustained and meaningful cross-group collaboration? They decided to talk to the program coordinator, who, while overwhelmed with the multiple demands of the job, was willing to listen to them and help in the identification of a possible response.

FRAMING OF THE PROBLEM

First-generation college students often struggle to find a place to which they belong on campus. The cultural expectations of the college environment and the social demands of engagement with high-SES peers can make them feel like outsiders. The creation of mentoring programs has been found to greatly enhance their sense of belonging on campus (Erickson, McDonald, & Elder, 2009). Mentoring programs oftentimes have both academic and social components. At the social level, they provide a space for students to be surrounded by those who have similar experiences, bond, and create networks of support. However, these positive outcomes can result in a distancing from the campus community.

Is it healthy for members of a mentoring program to stay within the realms of their comfort zone or should facilitators try to get them to connect with others?

QUESTIONS FOR DISCUSSION

1. Have you observed underrepresented groups of students be in competition with one another? Why does that take place?
2. Why do programs designed to serve specific groups of students become territorial at times? Are there any examples that you can think of?
3. What institutional mechanisms need to be in place in order for students to feel comfortable in all spaces on campuses?
4. Imagine that you are interviewing for a chief diversity officer position at the university referenced in the scenario above. A search committee member provides you with an overview of the issue and asks you to identify how you would respond. What would you say?
5. Despite the "open door" policy of many organizations and clubs, membership seems to be restricted to certain groups of students. How can this trend be counteracted?

Editors' Note: *This real-world experience has been altered to protect the identities of the people involved. The research project and the dialogues are fictitious.*

REFERENCE

Erickson, L. D., McDonald, S., & Elder, G. H., Jr. (2009). Informal mentors and education: Complementary or compensatory resources? *Sociology of Education, 82*(4), 344–67.

THIRTY-SIX

Antigay Slurs

One Student's Struggle

Kathy Previs

"Trent" always felt different as a child, though he could never quite explain exactly why. "While the other boys in my elementary school were concerned with monster trucks, Transformers, and sports, I was content playing with Barbie dolls, painting my nails, and putting on long T-shirts pretending I was Belle from *Beauty and the Beast*. I even remember having feelings for boys in my classes, but it was several years later before I heard the word 'gay' or knew what it truly meant," he said in an email interview.

Growing up in a small, rural town in a politically and religiously conservative state, being gay was not something that was talked about and, if it was, it was almost always in a negative manner. Trent's father, a drug addict and alcoholic who has been in and out of jails and rehabs for most of Trent's life, forced him into playing sports to "toughen him up," but none of it worked and that further caused a rift between him and his father.

To compound matters, as kids in Trent's grade school grew older, they started getting meaner, and Trent remembers being called "fag" in the hallways on many occasions. Being small and skinny, Trent lacked the confidence to stand up to them, especially because he did not want his secret to be revealed. This was for good reason. Once he did "come out," he was teased, bullied, and tormented.

"High school graduation finally arrived, and I was relieved to get away from the people who had made my life hell for so long. My parents did not attend college, but I had high hopes that this would bring a world of new people into my life—people who were also gay and knew what I was going through," Trent explained.

On the flip side of this, the university town where Trent attended college is also small and conservative, and many people were still judgmental toward homosexuals. "Preachers" stop outside of the student union building, holding signs with "God Hates Fags" and other antigay slurs, but because this is a free speech zone, they are allowed to do so legally. According to Trent, "it was upsetting to say the least, and it opened my eyes to just how much hatred for LGBT individuals existed in the world."

Also upsetting was the fact that other students, who also came to this same university to achieve a higher education, broadening their minds by meeting those from different backgrounds and interests, were as hateful and prejudged against homosexual students as those from neighboring small towns. Trent recalls one bullying instance in particular during his freshman year that made him especially uncomfortable.

"A person who I barely knew sent me a Facebook message telling me that, because I was gay, I was going to get AIDS and die—that is, unless someone ended up shooting me and killing me first. I was taken aback by the cruel words, but I had dealt with that for years and could move past it." Trent had been dealing with the hateful rhetoric of antigay slurs for quite a while. However, what many people do not understand is the physical and mental toll such remarks have on people over time.

To illustrate, Trent spoke about the physical and psychological effects of bullying at school, regardless of it being grade school or college.

> I was highly unprepared for the academic side of college—a side effect of being raised in a small town where education was undervalued and sports received the adoration. I struggled to juggle new friendships, attending classes, homework, and relationships, and the panic attacks soon returned. On top of all that, the first relationship I ever had, which began at the beginning of college, was a toxic one. The boy was a heavy drinker and ended up having his stomach pumped in his dorm room because of all the alcohol he consumed. I ended things with him, and he soon spiraled out of control—slashing the residence hall coordinator's tires and getting expelled from the university. Another boy I started seeing overdosed on drugs and passed away, so I visited the on-campus doctor and was prescribed Paxil for what the doctor called generalized anxiety disorder. The medicine made me feel nothing— like I was constantly in a fog—so I stopped taking it shortly thereafter.

Luckily, most college students can return home during breaks and summers and have the support of family. However, for Trent, this was not an option with some family members. "I was grateful to have friends and a mother who supported me unconditionally, but having no one who had experienced this to turn to was not easy. I came out to my father shortly thereafter, and he told me that I was the biggest disappointment of his life. While this was difficult to hear, our relationship was already so strained that it certainly was not surprising. To this day, we do not talk about me being gay."

Thankfully, Trent discovered that his university had a PRIDE Alliance on campus to help him cope with such matters. PRIDE Alliance is a group for LGBT individuals and their straight allies to gather in a safe space to talk about issues and causes important to them. PRIDE is an acronym for People Recognizing Identities and Differences for Equality. Trent recalled that it was refreshing to be around people who could relate to what he was experiencing.

"The older students in the PRIDE Alliance taught me so much about LGBT causes, issues, and equality while also providing new friendships and supporters. This place was my solace for the beginning of my college experience and I know that, without PRIDE Alliance, I would not be the person I am today," Trent said.

It is important that college campuses protect the rights of gay individuals. PRIDE Alliance and other organizations offer support and services to mitigate antigay slurs and educate all associated with life on a college campus. Evidently, the attention to antigay slurs and educating people on gay rights is working, though there is much more work to be done.

For example, as Trent recalled the Facebook message incident, a few years later, he received another message from that same person who bullied him, this time apologizing, saying he was upset by the way he had acted many years ago. He realized his anger came from a place of ignorance and wanted to make sure he made amends with Trent.

"That specific moment has stuck with me, because it affirmed what I had heard for so long: Fear is a product of ignorance. There is power in knowledge and, by understanding what someone else goes through, you cannot only move past your fear but also learn a skill that is so desperately needed: empathy," he added.

FRAMING THE PROBLEM

In this case study, we examined three areas from which gay college students hear antigay slurs: from strangers exercising their right to free speech, from other students, and from family members. The problem is how to respond to and prevent such slurs.

DISCUSSION QUESTIONS

1. Did Trent do the right thing by ignoring the college student who messaged him on Facebook with his antigay slurs? Should Trent have responded, or do you think his silence made the student eventually come around and apologize?

2. Although you hold your beliefs strongly that bullying and antigay slurs are wrong, you also recognize the fact that antigay slurs are protected speech. Therefore, how do you combat groups who visit college campuses that preach hate? Do you confront them? How do you educate them?

3. Do you agree with Trent's assessment that "fear is a product of ignorance"? Why or why not? Think about a time when you educated someone who changed his or her mind on something about which he or she was ignorant.

4. Knowing that many college freshmen share the same struggles as Trent, what advice would you give to a friend who confides in you that he or she experiences antigay slurs on his or her college campus?

5. While PRIDE Alliance and other groups help people cope with LGBT issues on college campuses, how would you suggest students like Trent educate members of their own families when they hear antigay slurs or hear negative messages such as being "disappointed" because of one's sexuality?

Editors' Note: *This case study is based on the real experiences of a college student, whom we have named here as Trent in order maintain his identity. The experiences are shared with his permission.*

THIRTY-SEVEN

Diversity and Student Media

Does the Faculty Advisor Have a Racist Agenda?

Tamara Zellars Buck

The Signal is a student-run, weekly newspaper at a predominantly White four-year university in the Midwest. *The Signal* has published for nearly a century under the direction of student editors and a faculty advisor.

The paid staff consists of a dozen student editors and advertising managers who are responsible for all aspects of production, including assigning, pitching, and writing stories, taking photos, laying out pages, maintaining a website, selling and creating ads, and promoting the newspaper online.

The faculty advisor serves as *The Signal*'s budget manager and contest coordinator and is responsible for training the editors and providing legal and ethical guidance related to publications. All final editorial decision making rests with the student editors.

Although the newspaper is run by students, it provides an experiential learning opportunity within the university's Department of Mass Communications journalism curriculum. As such, approximately 50 journalism majors in beginning and advanced newswriting and visual journalism courses must attend weekly staff meetings, take writing or photo assignments from editors, and submit work completed on deadline separately to editors for publication and to faculty for a class grade.

Dr. John Wilson, an untenured assistant professor of journalism, is in his fourth year of teaching and a new faculty advisor for *The Signal*. He earned his undergraduate degree in journalism at the university and was the newspaper's first Hispanic editor during his junior year 15 years ago. He teaches a variety of journalism courses and core curriculum courses that all mass communication majors must take.

The Signal's staff has historically not been diverse, and its coverage of events sponsored by people of color or international students has always been poor. As a student editor, Dr. Wilson sought to increase *The Signal's* inclusiveness by ensuring the coverage of cultural programming, especially events sponsored by African-American student organizations. Although working at *The Signal* was voluntary for journalism majors at the time, he also persuaded several African-American students to join the staff so that he could increase diversity in the types of stories pitched and covered, and in the use of African Americans as sources.

In his new role as faculty advisor, Dr. Wilson has realized that *The Signal* still has a problem with inclusiveness. In August, he noticed the first newspaper of the year did not have any photos or stories featuring a person of color. The second newspaper included a story about the university's achievement in enrolling over 1,000 international students for the semester, but the story's accompanying photo showed only the building that housed the International Student Program's office. There were no other stories featuring people of color as sources or in any photos, including a weekly Man-on-the-Street photo column.

None of *The Signal's* paid staff is a person of color this year. Although the expanded staff includes five African Americans who are enrolled in journalism courses, Dr. Wilson has noticed that those students always sit as a group in the back of the room and rarely interact with their White peers. Whenever editors ask for story ideas and pitches, the African-American students remain silent and rarely offer input on stories or potential sources other than to take assignments.

Dr. Wilson wants to inspire the staff to be more inclusive in its coverage and use of ethnically diverse sources. During a weekly meeting prior to publication of the third paper of the year, he asked the editors to critique their first two issues. The students identified several technical problems (grammatical, spelling, and AP style errors, and photo cropping and design mistakes) that should have been caught, but they were pleased with their efforts overall.

Dr. Wilson pointed out the fact that every photo in the first issue was of a White student or faculty member. "This was your Back to School issue," he said. "You had an entire photo page of people moving in and attending special events, and there's not one black or brown face. How is that even possible?"

Wilson then drew their attention to the international student enrollment story. When he mentioned their failure to use any persons of color as sources or photo subjects for the story, editors agreed that they should have spoken to international students. However, they also offered a possible justification for their failure to include a photo that featured an international student with the story.

The news release was released Friday morning, news editor Tonya Wellington explained. The paper was sent to the printer Tuesday morning, and they did not have enough time in the interim to find students who would consent to a photograph.

After hearing Wellington's explanation, editor-in-chief Dave Logan agreed that the lack of a person-focused photo was unfortunate. However, he said, the staff shouldn't go out of its way to find minority sources for stories or photos in the name of diversity.

"I don't think it's even ethical to try and cherry-pick a set number of minorities for our paper," Logan said. "We usually rely on the normal administrators and student leaders as sources for news stories. It's not our fault none of those people are Black."

Dr. Wilson ended the discussion at that point because he didn't want to be seen as argumentative with the staff so early in their new relationship. He also feared if he pushed too hard on the issue of diversity, students would complain and he would be removed as faculty advisor, something that might negatively impact his future tenure application. Instead, he encouraged the editors to be more cognizant of the need for inclusion, and he waited to see if any changes would result in the next issue of *The Signal*.

The third print edition again failed to include the use of people of color as sources or in any photos. Dr. Wilson noted that the weekly Man-on-the-Street column, which presents an excellent opportunity to visibly include people from different backgrounds in the newspaper, included a photo and comment from Smith Carruthers, a White transgender student activist and popular member of the student senate. All other photos and comments once again appeared to be of White students from around campus.

Dr. Wilson asked his beginning journalism class to critique *The Signal* at the beginning of their next class. Like the editors, the students caught a few technical problems, but no one independently noticed a lack of diversity in the sources or photos. When he asked specifically about the failure to include any people of color, Danielle Loftis, a sophomore and African American, raised her hand.

"Everyone knows *The Signal* won't talk to us," Loftis said, sounding disgusted. "That's why we don't read the paper." Two other African-American students nodded their heads in agreement with Loftis.

In the next editorial staff meeting, Dr. Wilson again brought up *The Signal*'s lack of diversity in its sources and photos. This time, he pointed out stories that could have easily incorporated minority sources, including one about the opening of a new restaurant in the food court, and another about how changes to the state's teacher licensure program would impact the university's curriculum for education majors.

"How hard is it to walk up to a person of color on this campus and ask their opinion about something as simple as their feelings about a new restaurant?" he asked. "It's like you're invisible on this campus—at least as far as *The Signal* is concerned—if you're not White."

Dr. Wilson then shared what he had learned from Loftis and her peers. Their comments received an angry response from the staff. "If they feel that way, why are they working here?" Logan asked. "They never say anything during the meetings, so I don't think they should get to complain about our coverage."

Sports editor Tommy Long offered a suggestion he thought might improve diverse coverage and lessen feelings of exclusion among African-American students.

"I was planning to do a feature story on Josh Williams, the quarterback on the football team," Long said. "He's a pretty cool guy, and they just won a game. Maybe that will show them that we're trying to do better."

The issue of diversity was dropped, and the meeting continued. Afterward, Dr. Wilson noticed several editors seated around Logan's desk having a quiet conversation. He decided to allow them some privacy and left the building.

Two days later, Dr. Wilson was called into the Department of Mass Communications chairperson's office. There, he learned that a student editor had sent an email complaining about "Dr. Wilson's racist agenda at *The Signal*" and requesting that another professor be assigned as faculty advisor. "He's a good professor, but he doesn't get to have a say in what we write or who we interview. He's creating a race problem where one doesn't exist." The letter writer indicated that he or she was writing on behalf of the entire staff.

FRAMING THE PROBLEM

As a former editor at the publication, Dr. Wilson knows there is a historic failure to include people of color as sources or to cover cultural events sponsored by the university or student organizations. He addressed the issue in his role as student editor. Now he wants to use his new role as a faculty advisor to help the current staff acknowledge their lack of diversity and identify ways to make improvements. He is untenured and fears that any reassignment could negatively impact his ability to achieve tenure in the future.

The paid editorial staff is not diverse and does not independently recognize any problems in regard to a lack of diversity in its coverage. Several African-American students who are part of the unpaid reporting staff affiliated with the newspaper have indicated that the lack of diversity is generally acknowledged by African-American students on campus.

Although they are considered newspaper staffers, those students are not vocal in meetings and do not initiate coverage of stories they may be aware of that would involve or appeal to a primarily African-American audience.

When the faculty advisor first brought up the issue of inclusiveness, staff members excused their lack of diversity because of a time constraint and an overall lack of available leaders. Later, an editor appeared angered by the suggestion that the staff was seen as noninclusive and seemed to lay the blame on African-American students who failed to share information. The editor later wrote an email to the faculty advisor's supervisor accusing him of having a racial agenda and creating controversy where none existed.

DISCUSSION QUESTIONS

1. How do you feel about the criticisms shared in the email?
2. How should the department chairperson respond to the critical email? Should a new faculty advisor be assigned to *The Signal*?
3. Should the editor's refusal to acknowledge a diversity problem be addressed? How, and by whom?
4. Do you think a sports feature on the quarterback will make an impact on African-American students at the university?
5. Identify ways in which the staff could engage the African-American staffers to share stories that would increase diversity. How could they increase sharing from the broader community?
6. In what ways can a nondiverse staff assess its coverage of minority populations (racial/ethnic minorities, disabled persons, LGBTQ+ populations, women's sports, etc.)? What do you believe should be Dr. Wilson's next move to increase diversity in *The Signal*'s coverage?

Editors' Note: This case study represents a combination of real scenarios, but some of the details were changed to protect the identities of those involved.

THIRTY-EIGHT

Diversity and Student Media

When Protectionism Interferes with News Gathering

Tamara Zellars Buck

The *Gateway Register* is a semiweekly newspaper at Gateway State University, a four-year public institution with an enrollment of 18,000 located somewhere in the South. The newspaper is affiliated with the university's School of Media Arts, which offers undergraduate degrees in journalism (photo, broadcast, print), strategic communication, and filmmaking. Journalism majors who are enrolled in several staff classes produce the content for print and online editions. The newspaper is managed by professors within the school.

The university has had success over the past five years in recruiting international students to seek degrees in its business and agriculture programs. However, officials have also received increasing reports of intolerance in that same period, especially from students hailing from countries in the Middle East. The students have reported problems ranging from derogatory remarks and harassment to physical threats and vandalism.

One evening in October of this year, the university police responded to a report of vandalism in the parking lot of H Dorm. There they found two hijab-wearing female students from Saudi Arabia sitting in a parked car near the back of the parking lot. The car had been egged. The students said they discovered the damage to the car after they exited the dormitory, where they had met with classmates two hours earlier to work on a group project.

"Go home terrorists!" had been written in the splattered mess on the car window.

In December, a group of four Indian students who had planned to sublease a house near the university from another student who was graduating

175

were informed the house was no longer available. The graduating student, who was White, told them he couldn't follow through with the sublease because "the landlord freaked when I told him where you were from."

When the students contacted the landlord directly, he told them the resident did not have permission to sublease the property and should not have made the deal. The house remained empty for the next two months.

University officials have documented but not publicized problems the international students have faced. In an effort to improve things, the university president has increased budgets for international student programming and instructed staff in the Office of International Programs to "protect those students at all costs."

The Office of Student Programs is charged with facilitating the recruitment and retention of international students at the university.

In March, the International Students Alliance announced it would host a senior prom to honor its graduating members on April 11. The event, which would be held in a ballroom on campus, would be cosponsored by the Office of International Programs. It was intended to be a gala affair that would feature food and music from the home countries of ISA members. It would be open to the public and could be attended by anyone who purchased a ticket.

Both ISA and the university heavily publicized the event via social media and campus mailings, and the *Gateway Register* ran a preview story publicizing the event to its readers.

Two weeks prior to the event, the *Gateway Register* received a news release from Christian Unity Chapel, a local church known for its fundamentalist ministry and intolerance for LGBTQ people and Muslims. The news release indicated that church members would protest the ISA's senior prom. They would be joined by Dennis Mathers, a high-profile extremist who became recognized for regularly leading activities to disrupt political and cultural events throughout the region.

Journalism faculty met after receiving the news release to determine how they should handle the information. Some wanted to immediately warn university officials, while others believed the best option was to ignore the information so as not to give the church a media platform. A third option they discussed was to use the news release as part of a bigger story analyzing increased aggressions against the international student population.

After much discussion, the faculty chose the third option and gave the story to Michelle Li-Wong, a senior who had covered the campus crime beat for much of the year. Li-Wong, a domestic student of Asian ancestry, had written a story about the car-egging incident when it occurred and had learned of the housing incident through mutual friends. She had planned to attend the ISA's senior prom with her boyfriend and several other friends who were also graduating that semester.

Li-Wong immediately called Deborah Morris, director of the campus news bureau, in order to schedule appointments with the university president, the international programs director, and the campus police chief. Li-Wong told Morris the subject of the interviews would be "protests at the ISA's upcoming senior prom and an increase in attacks on international students."

When Morris asked for more information, Li-Wong told her about the Christian Unity Chapel's planned protest. Upon learning that Dennis Mathers planned to attend, Morris gasped and told Li-Wong she would call her back before the end of the day.

Morris did not return Li-Wong's call. When Li-Wong made a follow-up phone call the next day, Morris told her the university would not be participating in the story.

"This is a big event for the ISA, and we don't want to scare people away," Morris said. "We're asking the *Register* not to cover this story."

Li-Wong tried to change Morris's mind, but without success. "I'm sorry, but we have to protect our students," Morris said.

Li-Wong told her professors about her conversation with Morris, and they told her to contact ISA president Raya Maz and request an interview. She decided to make the interview request in person the next day. She and Maz had taken a course together the previous semester, and she knew Maz could be found most afternoons doing clerical work in the Office of International Student Programs.

When Li-Wong arrived at the office, Maz was cordial and they shared small talk about their upcoming graduations. Just as Li-Wong was about to tell Maz about the story assignment and request an interview, international programs director Jim Clubbs walked out of his office and saw the two women.

"Don't talk to her, Raya," Clubbs said. "She's already been told we're not giving her a story." Clubbs told Li-Wong to leave his office and stop bothering his students. He then asked Maz to follow him into his office and shut the door.

Later that evening, a local television station broke the story that the Christian Unity Chapel planned to protest the ISA's event. A reporter broadcast live in front of a dormitory that housed a large number of international students, but no interviews were conducted with university officials. Only two White students appeared on camera for the story, and their comments suggested they felt bad for the international students but hoped the protest would not bring the campus any undue negative publicity.

Over the next two days, Li-Wong was continually stonewalled by university personnel and international student leaders. One student told her that ISA officers had contacted members and asked them not to talk to reporters about the senior prom or any incidents involving international students. Li-Wong shared this information with faculty at the *Gateway Register*, who contacted Morris and requested a meeting to discuss the matter further.

FRAMING THE PROBLEM

Gateway State University has actively and successfully recruited an international student population in recent years, but those students have increasingly become the victims of discriminatory and harassing behavior in the campus and local communities. After the most recent incidents, the university sought to improve campus life for these students by providing financial support for additional programming and urging staff to create a protective environment that shielded them.

The International Students Alliance and Office of International Programs announced plans to jointly sponsor a senior prom to honor international students graduating at the end of the semester. The programming was heavily promoted on campus and online, and the campus newspaper published a story about the event.

Two weeks before the event, a local church sent a news release announcing its intent to protest the senior prom. After some discussion, supervising faculty at the campus newspaper decided to assign a reporter to write a story that would include the protest as part of a broader story analyzing increased aggressions against the international student population.

Upon learning of the story's focus, the university's news bureau director refused to schedule interviews with university officials. She said her refusal was necessary to prevent disruptions to the scheduled event, and she asked the reporter not to cover the story. The reporter's attempt to interview the ISA president was stopped by a university official, and a no-talk order was apparently issued later that day to all international students through ISA.

Journalism faculty have scheduled a meeting to discuss the university's interference with the newsgathering process. In the meantime, the church's intent to protest has not been covered by the student newspaper and was broken by a local television station. The senior prom is less than a week away.

DISCUSSION QUESTIONS

1. At this point, what type of story should the *Gateway Register* publish and when? What information should be included or excluded? How should the story be sourced?
2. Li-Wong told Morris the subject of the interviews would be "protests at the ISA's upcoming senior prom and an increase in attacks on international students." Can you identify a better way to frame the story based on the faculty discussions?
3. The university seems to be taking a protectionist approach to the media in order to prevent them from exposing international students to potential harassment or unwanted attention. What are the benefits and problems of this type of policy?
4. How should the journalism faculty address the university's refusal to discuss the protest and incidents involving international students during the meeting? Should student reporters and ISA leaders attend the meeting?

Editors' Note: *This case study represents a combination of real scenarios, but some of the details were changed to protect the identities of those involved.*

About the Editors

Sherwood Thompson, Ed.D., has attained distinction through a lengthy and productive career, directing campus-wide diversity programs for three major Carnegie Foundation Division I public research universities, as well as one regional polytechnic university. In this capacity, he has worked as the assistant dean of the College of Education at Eastern Kentucky University, executive director of the Model Laboratory School and interim chief diversity officer, and he has held an array of leadership positions in departments that served the academic needs of diverse students, faculty, and staff. He is a professor in the College of Education at Eastern Kentucky University. He is the editor of two books—*Views from the Frontline: Voices of Conscience on College Campuses* and a two-volume *Encyclopedia of Diversity and Social Justice*—and he coedited *Coping with Gender Inequities: Critical Conversations of Women Faculty* with Dr. Pam Parry. He has published 60 articles, essays, and papers, all variously concerned with education reform and social justice, and 833 downloads through Encompass. His diversity and social justice training areas include faculty and staff diversity, inclusive excellence, sustainable diversity leadership, global citizen's awareness, school climate, equity and culture, organizational leadership, and appreciative inquiry.

Pam Parry, Ph.D., APR, is the chairperson of the Mass Media Department and associate professor at Southeast Missouri State University in Cape Girardeau. In 2016, she received the Applegate Award for Excellence in Research from the Kentucky Communication Association. She is the author of *Eisenhower: The Public Relations President*. She is the lead coeditor of a book series, Women in American Political History, which is being published by Lexington Books, a subsidiary of Rowman & Littlefield. She has freelanced for *the Baltimore Sun* and *The McLaughlin Group* television show. In 2009, she was named Teacher of the Year by an interest group within the Association for Education in Journalism and Mass Communication.

About the Contributors

Daria Lorio-Barsten, M.Ed., BCBA, LBA, is a project specialist at the Training and Technical Assistance Center at the College of William & Mary and a doctoral student in the Educational Policy, Planning, and Leadership Program at the College of William & Mary. She previously worked in a public-school setting with experiences as special education teacher, general education teacher, assessment and compliance coordinator, and instructional specialist in the department of accountability and instructional services in special education. In 2009, Lorio-Barsten received the Dean's Award for Excellence–Master's Level from the College of William & Mary. In 2007, she received the Outstanding Special Education Teacher Award from the National Association of Special Education Teachers. Her areas of interest encompass inclusive practices for students with disabilities, behavior management, data-driven decision making, and creativity.

Tamara Zellars Buck, J.D., M.S.A., is an associate professor and multimedia journalism coordinator in the Department of Mass Media at Southeast Missouri State University in Cape Girardeau. Since 2009, she has also served as faculty advisor to the *Arrow*, the university's award-winning student-run newspaper. She has worked professionally as a newspaper journalist and as a director of public relations for a not-for-profit corporation. In 2016, she was a cowinner of the College of Liberal Arts Outstanding Teacher Award for innovations in teaching Diversity in Communication. In 2013 she was named a Kopenhaver Fellow (inaugural class) by the Lillian Lodge Kopenhaver Center for the Advancement of Women in Communication in the School of Journalism and Mass Communication at Florida International University and the Commission on the Status of Women of the Association for Education in Journalism and Mass Communication (1 of 16 selected nationwide in an academic peer-review competitive process).

M. Kelly Carr, Ph.D., is an assistant professor and the basic course director in the Department of Communication at the University of West Florida. She is the author of *The Rhetorical Invention of Diversity: Supreme Court Opinions, Public Arguments, and Affirmative Action*, published by the Michigan State University Press. Other publications include a case study on the power of metaphor in legal arguments about health care, an examination of prudential legal argument, and a study of legal argumentation at the intersect of good faith, diversity, and academic freedom. She is working on a coauthored book about American town hall meetings, their shift from face-to-face to digital form, and the resulting implications on democratic deliberation for 21st-century Americans.

Doris W. Carroll, Ph.D., NCC, is associate professor within the Special Education, Counseling and Student Affairs Department at Kansas State University. There, she teaches graduate courses and conducts applied research in higher education administration, with emphasis in diversity, equity and inclusion, multicultural counseling, academic advising, and distance education. In November 2013, Dr. Carroll was awarded the Cultural Competency Award from the Kansas City chapter of the National Alliance for the Mentally Ill, or NAMI-KC, for her cultural competency workshops with Kansas City–area arts organizations. Her research interests involve racial microaggressions in online communication, and she recently coauthored a journal article on women faculty's experiences with gendered microaggressions in science, technology, engineering, and mathematics. She is a National Certified Counselor (NCC).

Nancy Chae, M.S., LCPC, NCC, NCSC, is a doctoral student in the Ph.D. program in counselor education and supervision at the College of William & Mary in Williamsburg, Virginia. She is a 2018 fellowship recipient for the National Board for Certified Counselors Minority Fellowship Program. She was a school counselor for six years in Baltimore City Public Schools at the pre-K–12 levels. She has additional experiences in school counseling curriculum development, high school admissions, and International Baccalaureate programming. She supervises master's level counseling students and is also a teaching intern for various master's level counseling courses. She is a licensed clinical professional counselor in Maryland, national certified counselor, and national certified school counselor.

Errick D. Farmer, Ph.D., serves as an assistant professor of professional leadership development at Florida A&M University, School of Business and Industry. Dr. Farmer holds a bachelor's of science in communication business from Florida State University, as well as a master's degree in applied social science, with a concentration in public administration and a doctor of philosophy in educational leadership, both from Florida A&M University. Dr. Farmer's research interests include mentoring, graduation and retention, and higher education administration.

Adriel A. Hilton, Ph.D., is dean of students and diversity officer at Seton Hill University in Greensburg, Pennsylvania. Recently he served as director of the Webster University Myrtle Beach Metropolitan Extended Campus. As the chief administrative officer, he worked to implement programs and policies to achieve Webster University's overall goals and objectives at the extended campus. In the past, Dr. Hilton has served as chief of staff and executive assistant to the president at Grambling State University and assistant professor and director of the Higher Education Student Affairs program at Western Carolina University.

Mustapha Jourdini, Ed.D., is a Moroccan-American and current director of the Center for International Student Programs and Services at Lamar University. He has developed a sensitivity for cross-cultural communication. Among other international organizations, he is active with NAFSA, Association of International Educators, through presentations and trainings. Dr. Jourdini holds a bachelor's and a master's degree in English and a doctorate in educational leadership and policy studies, with a specialization in international education from Eastern Kentucky University. He has given many presentations on diversity, cross-cultural understanding, and interfaith dialogue. His published research examines the impact of international students and cultural stereotypes.

Kyung Hee Kim, Ph.D., is professor of educational psychology at the College of William & Mary. She has dedicated her life to researching creativity and innovators so that everyone can harness creative potential to achieve his or her dream. She has developed the online CQ (Creativity Quotient) to help individuals identify and maximize their creative strengths. It expands on the Torrance Tests with Dr. Kim's patented eye-tracking technology, which instantly evaluates user-generated drawings. Her big, crazy dream is to change the world through innovations by ending high-pressure, test-centric education. She revealed "The Creativity Crisis" in *Newsweek* (2010). To reverse this crisis, she published her 2016 book, *The Creativity Challenge: How We Can Recapture American Innovation*.

Kirsten LaMantia, Ph.D., LPC, NCC, is a nationally certified counselor, licensed professional counselor, and assistant professor of counseling and director of the Counselor Education Training Clinic at Southeast Missouri State University. She is the author of *Here I Am*, an experiential classroom aid for discussing diversity, privilege, and oppression within the field of counselor education. She has published and presented on topics such as intersectionality, social justice, feminist pedagogy, LGBTQ+ populations, and multicultural competence.

Antoine Lovell, LMSW, MPA, is a doctoral candidate in social work and social policy at Fordham University Graduate School of Social Work. In 2017, he was awarded a competitive public policy fellowship from the Association for Public Policy Analysis and Management (APPAM); in 2018, he was selected to participate in the Asa F. Hillard III and Barbara Sizemore Research Course on African Americans and Education. Lovell's primary research interests are policy implementation, diversity in organizations, qualitative research methods, critical theory, youth development, homelessness, housing, race and racism, and poverty, along with social/public policy and their impact on people of African descent.

De'Andrea Matthews, D.R.E., is an author, educator, and national conference speaker. She has been an educator for more than 20 years, with experience at public and private institutions. She is director of the Office of Diversity and Inclusion at Wayne State University School of Medicine where she oversees the outreach, recruitment, and retention of students, faculty, and staff who are underrepresented in medicine. Dr. Matthews is also the president and book strategist for Claire Aldin Publications LLC.

Sarah M. Nuss, M.S., has served as the education coordinator for the Chesapeake Bay National Estuarine Research Reserve in Virginia (CBNERR) for the past 13 years. At CBNERR, Nuss leads the Education Program, which strives to enhance student, teacher, and public awareness, understanding, and appreciation of estuaries by providing hands-on, investigative field experiences, curriculum and information materials, teacher-training programs, and public outreach events. She has several publications related to marine science education and is pursuing a Ph.D. at William & Mary's School of Education in Educational Policy, Planning, and Leadership.

Eleni Oikonomidoy, Ph.D., is associate professor of multicultural education and graduate director for the master's degree in equity and diversity in education at the University of Nevada, Reno. Her research interests are academic and social integration experiences of newcomer immigrant and refugee students; globalization, culture, and education; and culturally responsive and globally aware teaching. She teaches undergraduate and graduate classes for both preservice and in-service teachers.

Sue Hyeon Paek, Ph.D., is an assistant professor in the School of Psychological Sciences at the University of Northern Colorado. She received her

Ph.D. at the University of Georgia. Her research has its focus on assessment of creative thinking, implicit theory of creativity, and their educational implications. She has been honored being a part of the Society for the Psychology of Aesthetics, Creativity and the Arts division of the American Psychology Association as a recipient of the Barron Award, 2017.

Kathy Previs, Ph.D., is associate professor of communication at Eastern Kentucky University where she teaches public relations courses. She also teaches journalism at West Virginia University, where she has been a graduate faculty member for WVU's integrated marketing communication program. Dr. Previs has published numerous articles on science communication, social media, presidential rhetoric, and public relations ethics and pedagogy. In 2015, she received the Applegate Award for Excellence in Research from the Kentucky Communication Association. She is diversity and inclusion liaison and the immediate past president of the Thoroughbred Chapter of Public Relations Society of America. She is the past president of the Kentucky Communication Association.

Leah Robinson, Ph.D., is the director of academic support in the Office of Diversity and Inclusion in the School of Medicine at Wayne State University. A lifelong learner who is passionate about education and technology integration, she is also the operations manager for COOL (Creative Online Opportunities for Learning) Technologies, L3C, an educational training and curriculum provider.

Sean Schofield is an assistant director of William & Mary's Cohen Career Center. He is pursuing a Ph.D. in education policy, planning, and leadership from William & Mary. He holds a master's degree in counseling from Montclair State University. His research interests include feminism and equity issues in higher education and the role values play in career satisfaction. Schofield has been an adjunct faculty member at Montclair State University, teaching family and child studies courses, and has been a guest speaker at several universities and business groups throughout New Jersey, New York, and Virginia.

Sherwood Thompson, Ed.D., has attained distinction through a lengthy and productive career, directing campus-wide diversity programs for three major Carnegie Foundation Division I public research universities, as well as one regional polytechnic university. In this capacity, he has worked as the assistant dean of the College of Education at Eastern Kentucky University, executive director of the Model Laboratory School and interim chief diversity officer, and he has held an array of leadership positions in departments that served the academic needs of diverse students, faculty, and staff. He is a professor in the College of Education at Eastern Kentucky University. He is the editor of two books—*Views from the Frontline: Voices of Conscience on College Campuses* and a two-volume *Encyclopedia of Diversity and Social Justice*—and he coedited *Coping with Gender Inequities: Critical Conversations of Women Faculty* with Dr. Pam Parry. He has published 60 articles, essays, and papers, all variously concerned with education reform and social justice, and 833 downloads through Encompass. His diversity and social justice training areas include faculty and staff diversity, inclusive excellence, sustainable diversity leadership, global citizen's awareness, school climate, equity and culture, organizational leadership, and appreciative inquiry.

Willie R. Tubbs, Ph.D., is an assistant professor of communication at the University of West Florida, where he primarily teaches courses in journalism. He holds a doctorate of philosophy degree in mass communication from the University of Southern Mississippi, an M.S. in interactive media from Quinnipiac University, and a B.A. in journalism from Louisiana College. He has worked as both a print journalist and an athletics media relations specialist.

Holly Wagner, Ph.D., LPC, NCC, is an assistant professor in the Department of Psychology and Counseling at Southeast Missouri State University. She is a certified school counselor, a nationally certified counselor, and a licensed professional counselor in Missouri. Dr. Wagner has previous work experience as a professional school counselor in a K–8 school setting, the program leader for the school counseling tract at Montana State University, and an assistant professor at the University of Missouri–Saint Louis.

Ginny Whitehouse, Ph.D., is a professor of broadcasting and electronic media at Eastern Kentucky University. She has more than 20 years of experience teaching and researching in the fields of media ethics. She has extensive experience working with a range of diverse student populations: from first-generation university students, urban centers, and remote mountain communities to elite honors students and graduate students. She served as a Fulbright Scholar at Sofia University in 2018, as well as guest lecturing at multiple universities and conducting international media interviews on misnaming fake news. She is Cases and Commentaries editor for the *Journal of Media Ethics* and has held national posts for the Association for Education in Journalism and Mass Communication and the Society of Professional Journalists.

Sara Zeigler, Ph.D., helped found the College of Letters, Arts, and Social Sciences at Eastern Kentucky University, serving as the college's first dean. Prior to becoming founding dean, Zeigler served in a plethora of leadership positions at EKU, including director of women's studies, chair of the Department of Government, Title IX coordinator, and dean of University Programs. A political scientist, Dean Zeigler holds three degrees in the field: a B.A. from Reed College and an M.A. and a Ph.D. from UCLA. Even as dean, Zeigler remains active with the university's nationally ranked mock trial team. Additionally, she was the president of the American Mock Trial Association from 2008 to 2010. Her research examines gender politics and equality jurisprudence. She has been published in many journals, some of which include the *Journal of Political Science*, *Feminist Formations*, and the *Journal of Political Science Education*.

Made in the USA
Middletown, DE
14 January 2020